# Becoming Fluent

# Becoming Fluent

How Cognitive Science Can Help Adults
Learn a Foreign Language

Richard Roberts and Roger Kreuz

The MIT Press
Cambridge, Massachusetts
London, England

© 2015 Massachusetts Institute of Technology

MIT Press books may be purchased at special quantity discounts for business or sales promotional use. For information, please email special_sales@mitpress.mit.edu.

This book was set in Stone by the MIT Press. Printed and bound in the United States of America.

Library of Congress Cataloging-in-Publication Data is available.

ISBN 978-0-262-02923

10  9  8  7  6  5  4  3  2  1

We dedicate this book to our parents:

Michaela Whitaker and Richard Roberts

and Paul and Ila Kreuz

# Contents

# Prologue

Adulthood is the perfect time to expand one's horizons through the study of other languages. All too often, however, the pleasure that should be inherent in learning to speak another language is marred by negative thoughts and experiences—past and present, real and perceived. As a result, we wrote this book for adults of all ages who want to study a foreign language but don't know where to begin.

Growing older confers on adults knowledge and abilities that more than offset any age-related decline. Through this book, we strive to show adult foreign language learners how to take advantage of their considerable strengths. To do so, we have drawn upon relevant research from cognitive science, as well as our own experiences teaching, conducting research, learning languages, and working and traveling abroad. Nothing would give us greater pleasure than to know that this book has encouraged adults to think about the advantages that only experience can bestow, and then to apply those advantages to language learning.

# Acknowledgments

There are many people to whom we owe a debt of gratitude for their assistance with this book. All readers, however, should be grateful to Andrew Garen, whose expert advice made the book more readable (and shorter). Gina Caucci's thoughtful editing saved us from many embarrassing errors, big and small. Alyssa Blair, David Kovaz, and Monica Riordan kindly gave us helpful suggestions. We also thank Cierra Wilson, who crafted the cognitive science starfish that appears as figure 1.1. Thomas Santos advised us on pedagogy from the perspective of English as a Second Language. We also thank Welcome Kim for allowing us to share his language-learning experiences. Richard Blackwood gets all the credit for the Sherpa analogy, which he graciously allowed us to steal. Jeonghoon Lee deserves thanks for refusing to teach Richard how to swear in Korean and for making sure Roger saw more of Korea than just downtown Seoul. Rick Marcus's teaching acumen and steadfastness as a friend more than make up for his ability to beat Roger at Scrabble. At the Foreign Service Institute (FSI), without the heartfelt enthusiasm of Priscilla Lujan, Doug Gilzow, Lauren Russell, and Mary Kim, this book might never have left the ground. We would also like to thank Leslie Barrett and Alexi Kral, whose feedback after reading the manuscript was a source of optimism and motivation in the final stages of compiling the book. We also thank Michele Trahan, of Old Orchard Beach, Maine, whose hospitality and encouragement we greatly value.

In Seoul, Keunhyun Shin and Inseop Lee were charitable with their praise, smiling through clenched teeth as Richard butchered Korean. Thanks also go to Richard's teachers at FSI's field school, Soon Kwak, Young Hee Lee, Yoon Jean Lee, and Hea Park Sung, who are caring and dedicated educators personally invested in the success of all their students. Tahk Sooyean deserves special mention for the gallons of coffee she drank Saturday afternoons, helping Richard prepare for his Korean language exam. In Okinawa, Momoe Miyagi took it upon herself to mentor Richard during his Japanese immersion trip. And many years ago Erica Urena's love of Portuguese ignited Richard's passion for it too. In Tokyo, Yoshihiro Kitagawa never tired of Richard's endless questions about Japanese language and culture. Fumiko Ito was more than Richard's sensei; she brought him into her family. Portugal could have no finer representatives than Kimon Oppermann and Alexandre Marques da Cruz, whose love of the Portuguese language, inquiring spirit, and goodness to all make them beloved teachers and friends. In Brazil, Angelica Monnerat personified dedication in teaching. In the Korean language department at FSI, Eunice Kim, Jessica Welter, Chung Ha, Yeonmi Bae, Sun Il Kim, Chris Song, and Kookhee Park made learning Korean fun and interesting at bathhouses, restaurants, parties, coffee shops, and even in the classroom. In the Japanese department, Yoshie Zorn, Kenichi Haramoto, Meiko Inouye, Masako Nanto, Miyuke Tsuchiya, and Setsuko Okabe deserve credit for bringing Richard's Japanese up to a level fit for proper society. Tyrone Parker showed inexhaustible patience over long evenings spent helping

Richard with his French. Greg Morgan's love of language curiosities and wordplay never fails to entertain, and was responsible for our learning about the Unspeakableness project. And because Jeff Newbern is both a skilled teacher and such a generous friend, several examples from his classes now grace this book.

Roger would like to thank his teachers of German: Eric Paderi, Sherri Gruber Wagner, and Marianne Bigney. Jason Braasch and Jenny Roche made helpful suggestions that are greatly appreciated. For their support and encouragement through all phases of the writing of this book, he is especially grateful to his department chair, Frank Andrasik, and Laura Simpson, his administrative assistant. And for his role in turning a terrified twenty-one-year old into an experimental psycholinguist, Roger acknowledges his huge debt to Sam Glucksberg.

Finally, at the MIT Press, we are indebted to Senior Editor Philip Laughlin and Acquisitions Assistant Christopher Eyer for believing in this project and bringing it to fruition. Without Judy Feldmann's deft editing, the book would be much less comprehensible. We also thank three anonymous reviewers whose comments on the proposal greatly sharpened our thinking on this topic. Because Richard works for the US Department of State, he would like to make clear that the contents of this book are his opinions and not those of the US government. Any errors of fact, omission, or commission are entirely Roger's ... just kidding—they are Richard's, too.

Richard and Roger
Memphis, Tennessee
August 2014

# About the Authors

**Richard Roberts's** educational background spans the speech and hearing sciences, clinical psychology, and experimental psychology. After earning his doctorate at the University of Memphis, he was a postdoctoral researcher at the National Center for Health Statistics. He spent twelve years teaching psychology in Europe and Asia with the University of Maryland University College. During that time, he achieved varying degrees of proficiency in German, Portuguese, and Japanese. Since 2006, he has been a US diplomat, serving at embassies in Niger, Japan, and South Korea. He has also studied French, Japanese, and Korean at the US Department of State's Foreign Service Institute. He currently works in the Public Affairs Section of the US Embassy in Seoul.

**Roger Kreuz** has been a professor of psychology for over twenty-five years. After studying psychology and linguistics at the University of Toledo, he earned his doctorate at Princeton University, and was a postdoctoral researcher in cognitive gerontology at Duke University. He has published on topics in the psychology of language, primarily in text and discourse processing and figurative language. His research has been funded by the National Science Foundation and the Office of

Naval Research. He has coedited two books: *Empirical Approaches to Literature and Aesthetics* and *Social and Cognitive Approaches to Interpersonal Communication*. He has been a student of German and Old English, but his progress in the latter has been hampered by a lack of native speakers to practice with. He currently serves as an associate dean at the University of Memphis.

# 1   Terms and Conditions

If people knew how hard I had to work to gain my mastery, it wouldn't seem wonderful at all.

—Michelangelo

When you meet someone who speaks a foreign language well, you may attribute her skill in the language to natural ability.[1] This is probably because you don't know about all the hard work that went into achieving this level of mastery. But with the exception of certain people we might call savants, anyone who has ever learned another language as an adult did so only as the result of real effort. In that way, this book is most assuredly not a quick fix. But if you apply the specific skills and abilities you have honed over a lifetime, learning a language can be fun and rewarding. The older you are, the more tools in your toolbox you can take advantage of to reach your goal. Everyone possesses unique sets of skills and abilities that can be applied to language learning—if they can get past some false beliefs. It is to these that we now turn.

## Three Myths about Foreign Language Learning

From the very beginning of Richard's Korean language study, he felt frustrated with his progress. It seemed as if no matter how hard he tried, he was not advancing fast enough. His teachers were constantly encouraging him to study harder and to memorize more. He knew that he was working hard—studying for class, meeting with native Korean speakers for language exchange, watching videos, and learning Korean songs. At first, he thought he had hit the age wall. Richard had been successful when he had studied German, Portuguese, French, and Japanese, but he began the study of Korean at age fifty-two, and he thought that perhaps he was now too old to take on another language. Certainly, according to conventional wisdom, he should not expect much progress.

One day, he was having coffee with his Korean language exchange partner (who has the inviting name "Welcome"). Richard wondered out loud whether Welcome felt his English had improved since coming to the United States. It certainly seemed to Richard that Welcome's English had gotten better, and Richard was expecting Welcome to tell him that he thought so too. Instead, Welcome said he didn't know. When Richard asked him what his teachers thought, Welcome replied that because American teachers always compliment students, he couldn't trust what they told him. Welcome went so far as to wish that his teachers would be more critical. For Welcome, the more they criticized, the more they showed that they were interested in his progress.

This was an eye-opening conversation for Richard. From then on, he realized that his perceived lack of progress in Korean was a function of his own expectations about what it means to be a successful language learner. Richard had been measuring his progress by how much he didn't know. He saw the glass as half empty, and therefore pushed himself to memorize more and more material. But relying on rote memory alone is the second-worst thing any adult foreign language learner can do.

Of course, memorization is required to learn a foreign language; however, rote memorization exercises (such as listening to a text and then parroting it back verbatim, memorizing long passages of dialogue, slogging through flashcards) place the adult learner at a disadvantage cognitively. Because this ability declines with age, placing too much emphasis on rote memory can lead to frustration, is demoralizing, and can ultimately cause any adult language learner to quit.

You may be wondering, if rote memorization is the second-worst thing for an adult learner, what is the worst? It is the belief that one is too old to learn a foreign language. The next thing we want to do, therefore, is to dispel this, and two other myths that surround language learning in adulthood.

*Myth 1: Adults cannot acquire a foreign language as easily as children.*

On the contrary, there is evidence to suggest that adults can learn new languages even more easily than children. There are only two areas where children may be superior to adults when it comes to language learning. The first appears to be their ability to acquire a native accent. It is certainly the case that normal adults are capable of achieving native-like fluency as well. But even if an adult language learner is more likely to speak with an accent, there is no reason to be overly pessimistic about it, as long as it does not interfere with intelligibility. Children's other advantage over adults is that they have no language learning anxiety. In other words, because children aren't burdened by a belief that they cannot learn a language, they are free from such self-defeating thoughts.[2]

*Myth 2: Adults should learn foreign languages the way children learn languages.*

Children's brains and adult brains are different. Therefore, why would anyone expect that the same teaching techniques that work for children be appropriate for adults? They aren't. But, unfortunately, adult language learners sometimes try to learn a language by stripping away all of the strategies and learning experiences that helped them become successful adults in the first place. They try to learn a foreign language "purely," the way they acquired their first language. This isn't possible. Trying to do so inevitably leads to frustration and a higher probability of abandoning the goal. A more fruitful approach would be for adults to build on their considerable cognitive strengths and to not envy or try to mimic children's language learning.

*Myth 3: When learning a foreign language, try not to use your first language.*

Some adult language learners believe that they should never, ever, translate from their first language to their target foreign language. But this advice deprives adult language learners of one of their most important accomplishments—fluency in their native language. Although it is true that one language is not merely a direct translation of another, many aspects of one language are directly transferable to a second language. It's not even possible to completely ignore these aspects, and trying to do so can be frustrating.

For example, an English-speaking adult who is learning Portuguese could hardly avoid noticing that the Portuguese word to describe something that causes harm in a gradual way, *insidioso*, is suspiciously like the English word *insidious*. It would make no sense to pretend as if prior language skill in English is not transferable in this case. It is true that such cognates are not found between all languages and are sometimes inaccurate (as in wrongly equating the English word *rider* to the French word *rider*, which means "to wrinkle"). Nonetheless, looking for places where concepts, categories, or patterns are transferable is of great benefit, and also points out another area where adult foreign language learners have an advantage over children.

Regrettably, any of these myths could prevent even the most highly motivated adult from embarking on a language learning journey. However, there is a great deal of research that addresses such false beliefs. Insights from the field known as cognitive science offer guidance that is directly relevant to the adult foreign language learner.

### What Is Cognitive Science?

Cognitive science is an interdisciplinary movement that began in the 1960s and became highly visible as a scientific enterprise during the 1970s. Cognitive science occupies the intersection of a number of fields in which researchers from many disciplines explore questions about the nature of mind. The disciplines centrally involved in this endeavor include psychology, linguistics, philosophy, neuroscience, artificial intelligence, and anthropology.[3] The field of education is now commonly included as well (see figure 1.1).

As a scientific movement, cognitive science is notable because it represents a deliberate shift away from extreme specialization. Cognitive scientists actively promote inclusivity and the adoption of new points of view, and this cross-fertilization has produced hundreds of important new research programs. It is still the case, however, that cognitive scientists are generally trained in one of the specific disciplines shown in figure 1.1.

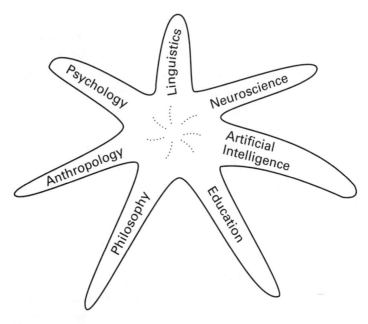

**Figure 1.1**
We chose the seven-armed starfish (*Luidia ciliaris*) to illustrate the field of cognitive science. Like the arms of a starfish, no one branch of cognitive science is more important than another. The arms must work in concert for the starfish to move. There is no head or tail, but all of the arms radiate from a "central executive."

For example, Richard and Roger were trained as psycholinguists in experimental psychology programs; however, they are also cognitive scientists because their graduate training emphasized cognitive science and their research and ideas are influenced by these related disciplines.

Before discussing how cognitive science relates to adult foreign language learning in more depth, we first need to define some terms.

## Mind the Gap

In describing mental processes, cognitive scientists frequently categorize them as being either *top down* or *bottom up*. Top-down processes, which are also referred to as *conceptually driven* processes, utilize what you already know in service of perception and comprehension. For example, experts solve problems differently from novices because they have more knowledge and experience in a given domain.

Although top-down processing applies to cognition in general, it plays an important role in the comprehension of spoken language. The environments in which we speak to one another are rarely very quiet ones—think about the last time you met some friends for a meal in a restaurant. Even in a relatively quiet establishment, your conversational partners will be competing against background noise and the voices of other patrons. And if it were necessary for your ears to pick up every sound spoken by your dinner companions, you simply wouldn't be able to understand much of what they said—there is too much noise to contend with. Fortunately, the cognitive system is able to fill in the missing information, even without you being aware that this is happening. This is why background noise is more disruptive for beginning language students than it is for advanced students—without greater knowledge of the language, top-down processing can't fill in what's missing.

Although top-down processing is clearly very important, it's not the whole story. Bottom-up processing, which is also referred to as *data-driven* processing, is the opposite of top-down processing. This term refers to situations in which you perceive a stimulus without preconceptions or assumptions about what you're experiencing. Instead of being guided by expertise or familiarity, bottom-up perception depends solely on information that comes from your five senses. For example, vision and hearing are mostly bottom up until the brain can make sense of what was seen or heard. If you wear glasses, then you are correcting for a deficit in the data your eye must use in order for your brain to see. Glasses correct a bottom-up problem.

Virtually all language skills require the interaction of both top-down and bottom-up processing. Reading and understanding a short story is a good example of such an interaction. You need to decode the letters and words on the page, and match them against representations in long-term memory, which is bottom-up processing. However, you also have to make use of your knowledge of the characters' histories and motivations, and how stories work, which is very much top-down processing.[4]

Adult language learners excel at top-down processing because of their extensive world knowledge and experience. For example, because you already have an understanding of basic narrative structures (think of "boy meets girl, boy loses girl, boy gets girl back"), you can capitalize on your knowledge of these expectations while reading in ways younger readers may not be able.[5] As we get older, and our hearing and vision become less acute, savvy adult language learners will offset any such decline by drawing upon their greater world knowledge. Insights from cognitive science can show you how to do this.

**What Does "Meta" Mean?**

Before exploring how this research can help you learn a new language, it is necessary to introduce the concept of *meta*. Although the meaning of words like *cognition*, *memory*, and *linguistics* is fairly straightforward, you may not be familiar with the concepts of *metacognition, metamemory,* or *metalinguistics.* Let's look at what these are, and why they will be so important in the chapters that follow.

Metacognition, simply put, is thinking about thinking, and metamemory is thinking about memory. Most of the time, cognitive processes function so smoothly and effortlessly that we rarely pause to reflect on them. However, when we are fooled by an optical illusion, or try to understand a friend's failure to follow simple directions, or mishear what someone said, we may briefly stop and consider the way that our mind works (or momentarily fails to work). This is metacognition, and it is the greatest strength of adult learners.

It's not easy to infer what children know about their mental processes. Certainly their cognitive skills are improving all the time as they gain more experience in the world. As anyone who has children knows, the changes happen in leaps and bounds. However, the full range of metacognitive and metamemory abilities are not fully developed until adulthood.[6] This is hardly surprising, since young children haven't had enough experience with cognitive successes and failures to be able to make many generalizations based on these experiences. It's also the case that the consequences of poor memory in young children are rarely serious. Little kids have an incredibly sophisticated external memory device (better known as "mom" or "dad") to keep track of anything that the child must do or remember. If the child forgets or doesn't understand, mom or dad is there to help.

Adults, however, have developed a more sophisticated understanding of their cognitive processes, but it's not perfect and may vary by subject matter.[7] Adults have learned, for example, that they can memorize a seven-digit phone number, but not a twenty-digit package tracking number. They know that it's helpful to mentally rehearse directions that they are given, or to use strategies that make computer passwords easier to remember. But it may not be intuitive how metacognitive abilities can be applied to foreign language learning.

Metalinguistic awareness is somewhat different. It refers to knowing about how your language works, and not just knowing *a* language. Metalinguistics is not the history of the language, or knowing word origins, but rather knowing how to use language to *do* things: how to be polite, or to lie, or to make a joke. Once again, this is an area in which adults excel, even if they aren't really aware that they possess this knowledge. But no one is born with this skill—for example, it's been demonstrated that politeness routines are learned in childhood from parents, who ask for the "magic word" before their kids are allowed to excuse themselves from the dinner table.[8]

In adulthood, metalinguistic knowledge can be impressively precise. Knowing the difference between a clever pun and a groan-inducing one, for example, reflects fairly sophisticated metalinguistic awareness.

The good news about metacognitive skills is that you don't have to learn them all over again when you start learning a new language. Instead, you only need to take the metalinguistic, metamemory, and metacognitive abilities you've already developed in your native language and apply them to the study of your target language.

## 2   Set Yourself Up for Success

**Well Begun Is Half Done**

Well begun is half done.
—attributed to both Aristotle and Mary Poppins

Imagine an adult learner who has just enrolled in his first Japanese class. This student decides that the best way to learn the ninety-two modern written *kana* that represent the sounds of Japanese is to create a practice book. For each kana, he creates a separate page. At the top of the page he affixes a picture of the kana with a diagram showing the stroke order. The rest of the page contains uniform blank squares for writing practice. He arranges these sheets into two notebooks (one for *hiragana*, the other *katakana*) and creates attractive covers so that he can take the notebooks with him to practice whenever he has free time. The problem with this strategy is that he spends all his time preparing to study the kana—but not actually studying them. What he sees as good preparation is really wasted time (and paper). By the second week of class he lags behind the other students and ends up dropping the class midway through the term. Clearly, this student did not begin well. But what exactly went wrong?

When it comes to studying a foreign language, beginning well doesn't start on the first day of class or the first day in a foreign country. It starts with the decision to study the language: if this decision is not entered into wisely, the actual study of the language will be surprisingly difficult. Faulty decision making can cause students to question their abilities, which then leads to decreased motivation and consequently more struggling with the language. Such a downward spiral culminates in disappointment and disillusionment. Because cognitive scientists study how people make decisions, their research in this area can help with the decision on where, when, and how to study a foreign language. That is the best way to begin well.

Although some people make decisions by adding up perceived pros and cons in a loosely mathematical way, that approach doesn't work with complex decisions such as whether to start (or restart) studying a foreign language. As in most of life, when it comes to these kinds of decisions, there is no precise formula to guide us. Decisions on complex issues like studying a foreign language must be approached flexibly, because these decisions are invariably made in the absence of complete information. One reason for disappointment with foreign language learning is that the decision is often made without a realistic appraisal of what it will take to succeed—or without even knowing how to define success. Whether they know it or not, even for individuals who have successfully studied one foreign language, the decision to study another one still requires a good deal of forethought. But it is possible to master a "super hard" language like Chinese but not a "world language" like French—it happens more often than you'd expect.

Whenever people make decisions, big or small, in the face of such uncertainty, they rely on cognitive strategies called *heuristics*. These mental shortcuts, or rules of thumb, are "good enough" strategies that can be resorted to when a decision must be made in the face of unknown and unknowable information (which is most of the time). And often enough, using heuristics to make a decision is a smart option.

One very useful heuristic strategy is called the *availability heuristic*, which states that the more quickly and easily examples of a phenomenon can be generated mentally, the more common that phenomenon is likely to be. Let's try it. Which name is more common in the United States: Mary or Matilda? One way to answer this question would be to search the Internet for relevant statistics about baby names. But in this case you probably don't feel the need to do so, since you can come up with the right answer more quickly using the availability heuristic. You would probably say the name Mary is more common, since you can think of more people named Mary than you can think of people named Matilda. This is the beauty of the availability heuristic: it is quick, easy, and most of the time leads to an answer that is good enough for the circumstances. In case you doubt the power of heuristic strategies, they are generally so useful and so efficient that cognitive scientists who work in the area of artificial intelligence have long sought ways to teach computers how to take advantage of them.[1]

Unfortunately, like all heuristics, the availability heuristic is not foolproof. For example, people are more likely to buy earthquake insurance immediately *after* an earthquake. But they tend to drop coverage over time, because as the memory of the earthquake fades, the necessity of earthquake insurance seems less urgent—when in fact, the likelihood of an earthquake is actually increasing as time passes without one.[2]

The point here is not to avoid using the availability heuristic—that would be impossible. Rather, the point is that for all their strengths, heuristics have weaknesses that can sabotage the best-laid plans. This is especially true when it comes to studying a foreign language as an adult.

Related to the availability heuristic is the *simulation heuristic*, which works in much the same way, but which inadvertently can lead to frustration for the adult language learner. According to the simulation heuristic, the more quickly and easily you can create a mental scenario in which an event occurs, the more likely you will be to predict that the event will occur. For example, how likely is it that you will become president of the United States? To answer this question, you need to create a mental simulation in which you think about all the things that would have to happen for you to become the president: the more things that would have to happen, the more unlikely the outcome will seem to you. If you are like Roger or Richard, the possibility of becoming president will seem quite remote. If you are the vice president, it will seem less so.

As with the availability heuristic, to simulate becoming the president, you must access your memory for relevant information. As you do, you will be influenced by how quickly you can access this information from memory and also by how relevant it is to the scenario you are creating. Experiences that you recall easily and that seem similar to the present scenario will add to your confidence. For example, if you successfully ran for the governor of a state, you could more easily imagine a situation where you are elected president than if you had only successfully run for class treasurer in high school.

In the same way, deciding to study a foreign language requires visualizing what it will take to reach a desired level of competence. But once you decide to study a foreign language, if you don't reach your goal, is the reason that you, as an adult, have difficulties learning a foreign language, or could it be that the simulation heuristic failed you in some important ways? Let's explore some weaknesses in the simulation heuristic that, if avoided, can help better predict what it will take to successfully master a foreign language.

One reason a simulation does not always align with the actual outcome of an event is because of a trap called the *planning fallacy*.[3] The planning fallacy is the tendency to underestimate how much time, effort, or money it will take to accomplish a goal. This is because we tend to be overly confident about our ability to reach a goal and misjudge the resources that are required. One need only look at the nightly news to see examples of where the planning fallacy has derailed outcome expectations.

We become susceptible to a planning fallacy when we focus too much on the good things that will happen when we achieve a goal and not enough on the resources it will take for us to reach that goal. For example, in deciding to study a foreign language, you might think about how wonderful it will be to order food in a restaurant, flirt, or read a local newspaper. Thinking about outcomes can be motivating, but they should not form the core of the decision-making process. One way to avoid the planning fallacy, therefore, is to separate the reasons for *wanting* to master a language from the specific steps that must be accomplished in order to master it.

In a mental simulation, focusing on the process of what it will take to reach a goal results in better planning than focusing on the outcome of what will happen once the goal is achieved. Not only does such process-focused planning result in a greater probability of actually reaching the goal, it also reduces stress along the way.[4] In other words, in deciding whether or not to study French, think about how each day must be structured in order to find the time to study, rather than how great it will be to toss off witty *bons mots* at the café *Les Deux Magots*.

Another reason for incorrect planning when creating a mental simulation is the tendency to be overly optimistic about the outcome of events. The simulation is often based on an ideal situation where everything goes exactly as planned, without taking into consideration all of the things that could go wrong. For example, Richard decided to spend a month in Brazil studying Portuguese. He thought that a month would give him enough time to reach the level of mastery he needed to take a telephone test in Portuguese for the Foreign Service. To do this, Richard went to Rio de Janeiro, enrolled in a Portuguese language class, and was mugged the day he arrived. That certainly wasn't the fault of the Portuguese language, and it may in fact have been a good thing since he became more careful afterward, but he also spent more time in his hotel room and not out meeting people. Consequently, Richard did not improve his Portuguese as rapidly as he had expected, he did not pass the telephone test, and he had to spend another month studying in Brazil the following year. The moral of the story is not to avoid being mugged (though that is also good advice), but to expect the unexpected when charting a course of action. Doing so will lead to less frustration when things don't go as planned—and they won't.

Finally, because the simulation heuristic works well most of the time, when it doesn't, people blame their own abilities—or worse, those of others—rather than recognizing the real culprit: how the heuristic was used. Such blame may be reinforced by what is called *counterfactual thinking*, which is a mental simulation that occurs *after the fact* and focuses on what might have

been. For example, who do you think is happier to be standing on the winners' platform during the Olympics—the silver
medalist or the bronze medalist? Even though silver is higher
than bronze, the smile of the bronze medalist is usually much
brighter than that of the silver medalist. The bronze medalist
can easily create a simulation whereby she came in fourth; the
silver medalist can just as easily create a simulation whereby he
captured the gold.[5]

Once you've made the decision to study a foreign language,
some other heuristics can also adversely affect the outcome. One
of these is called *anchoring and adjustment*. This heuristic specifies
that it is difficult for us to move very far away from what we have
initially decided—even when the reality of the situation neces-
sitates a change in plans. For example, adult language learners
may slavishly follow a preset lesson plan (i.e., the anchor) even
when it becomes clear that it is not very effective. Although we
may make minor adjustments to plans when something is not
proceeding well, it is unlikely that we will make the kind of dras-
tic changes that are often needed. You probably know someone
who continued to create and study flashcards in order to memorize vocabulary words when, in fact, this strategy was not particularly effective. He might have adjusted the task by studying fewer
flashcards at a time, or by switching from index cards to an elec-
tronic format; however, he never considered simply abandoning
the anchor, that is, to stop using flashcards altogether.

A related error in decision making that can trip up even the
most dedicated language learner is the *confirmation bias*, which
happens when people give more credence to information that
confirms their beliefs, while at the same time ignoring or dis-
counting information that goes against these beliefs. The confirmation bias works against groups and individuals both in

planning and carrying out a course of action. By ignoring con-tradictory feedback, we lose the opportunity to make changes that could drastically improve the probability of success. It can be a problem of *Titanic* proportions, so to speak.

Consider the first myth of this book: *Adults cannot acquire a foreign language as easily as children.* Meeting an adult who tried but failed to learn a foreign language failure confirms the belief. Meeting an adult who succeeded is written off as a fluke, when in fact, plenty of people can and do successfully master a foreign language in adulthood.

The confirmation bias is at work in all kinds of stereotypes—take your pick. Once you know what to look for, it's easy to see, but it's not so easy to change. Interestingly, negative stereotypes about aging can affect more than just one's attitude about lan-guage learning; they can also affect one's health. For example, maintaining positive beliefs about aging is associated with fewer cardiovascular incidents.[6]

For all of their strengths, given the various ways heuristic strategies can fail, it's no wonder that highly motivated adults sometimes abandon their foreign language studies. They blame themselves or their teachers for the failure, when a lack of insight into the decision-making process set them up to fail in the first place. Perhaps saddest of all, once the decision to abandon for-eign language study is made, a final heuristic rears its ugly head: the hindsight bias. This is when they look back at the failure and say to themselves, "I knew it would happen all along."[7]

**Caution: Contents May Be Habit Forming**

If it's been a while since you were a student, you probably don't relish the prospect of developing study habits for learning a foreign language. However, just studying a little bit every day is one of the most efficient ways to allocate your time. Fortunately, the successful formation of habits is something that psychologists know a great deal about. Unfortunately, it is also something that is discussed in a very simplistic way in the media, so what you've heard about habit formation may not be entirely accurate. It is necessary, therefore, to start by addressing three questions about habit formation.

1. *Does it take twenty-one days to develop a new habit?*

In 1960, Maxwell Maltz, a plastic surgeon, published a book entitled *Psycho-Cybernetics: A New Way to Get More Living Out of Life*. In this book, he made the claim that a whole host of phenomena require twenty-one days in order to effect a change (e.g., "People must live in a new house for about three weeks before it begins to seem like home"). It's unclear how he arrived at this magic number for so many different things. Subsequent research, however, has shown that there is no preordained timetable required to form a new habit.[8] So don't think about study habits in terms of quantity—think about them terms of quality.

Try to incorporate your target language into your life as much as possible—but do it in a meaningful way. For example, there are language books that include vocabulary words on adhesive strips that can be attached to objects in your home. If you were studying Spanish, you might put the label for *la cuchara* ("spoon") next to the spoons in the kitchen drawer. That way, theoretically, each time you use a spoon you'd see this word and make the association. Unfortunately, many people might just read the label, and because it feels familiar ("Yes! *la cuchara* means 'spoon'!"); they don't realize that they are only thinking about the word in a superficial way that does not make the kind of associations that lead to long-term retention.

Rather than putting labels on all of the objects in your home or office, a better habit to develop would be to remind yourself for each object you encounter that it has an equivalent in your target language. Even better than putting a label next to the spoons, when you pull a spoon out of the drawer, ask yourself if you remember the Spanish word for spoon. If not, look it up, then think of a way to associate this word with other words in the target language. Once you start remembering the word consistently when you see the object, then start making sentences using the word, for example, *Necesito una cuchara para comer mis Corn Flakes*. This habit of thinking more deeply about the language will pay great dividends—and you won't have to wait twenty-one days to start seeing results.

2. *Do setbacks mean that you've failed?*

Despite the best of intentions, life events can interrupt consistent study habits. You may find yourself setting aside foreign language study for days or even weeks. This can be frustrating, but it doesn't mean that you should abandon your goals.

The development of new habits has often been studied in the context of smoking cessation. One of the best predictors of whether people are ultimately successful in giving up smoking is the number of times they've managed to quit before, if only for a few days or weeks.[9] So if you find yourself "falling off the wagon" of foreign language study, don't take it as a sign that you can't do it—hop back on that wagon and try again. Remember too that relearning is faster than learning, so whenever you do start again, you'll have a head start.

3. *If a little study is good, is a lot of study better?*

Call this the *fertilizer fallacy*: if a little bit of the stuff in this bottle will make my begonias grow faster, then why shouldn't I use all of it? The reason, as many gardeners have had occasion to learn, is that fertilizers contain soluble salts that cause root burn: the plants' ability to absorb water and other nutrients is reduced, and the plants become dehydrated, turn yellow, and wilt.

You don't want to give your brain root burn. Studies have consistently demonstrated that learning information a bit at a time, what cognitive scientists call *distributed practice*, is superior to *massed practice*, which is just another term for cramming.[10]

## Suggestions for Developing Effective Language Study Habits

1. *Determine what is realistic.*

It might seem obvious that it is important to set goals in life. Everywhere you look, you are encouraged to "Aim High" or "Reach for the Stars." Those are fine sentiments, but the real question is how? Cognitive scientists have long studied goal-setting behavior. The ongoing research was summed up by Edwin Locke and Gary Latham, who wrote: "Specific, high (hard) goals lead to a higher level of task performance than do easy goals or vague, abstract goals such as the exhortation to 'do one's best.' So long as a person is committed to the goal, has the requisite ability to attain it, and does not have conflicting goals, there is a positive, linear relationship between goal difficulty and task performance."[11]

Locke and Latham's conclusion would seem to bode well for the adult language learner. Clearly, learning a foreign language is difficult, but most adult language learners who are committed to this goal have the requisite ability to attain it, as long as they keep conflicting goals from interfering. Why then do so many adult language learners end up feeling frustrated or disappointed or dissatisfied with their language learning experience? How can you keep this from happening to you?

If your goal is to achieve native-like fluency in a "super hard" language like Chinese or Arabic by the end of the year, you may be setting yourself up for failure. A goal like that is virtually impossible to achieve, so it would be very difficult to figure out a plan of study for attaining it. You're much better off setting realistic, short-term goals over a period of time as a way to accomplish the long-term goal. If you can achieve these subgoals, you'll be more motivated to stick with your plan of study as time goes on.

2. *Go public with your goal.*

Once you've settled on a goal that is realistic, it can be highly motivating to share it with others. If you simply toy with the idea of undertaking foreign language learning, you may never get around to starting. If you share your goal with your spouse, or a friend or sibling, they're likely to inquire periodically about your progress. It would be embarrassing to keep telling them that you haven't even begun, so this can be another form of motivation.

3. *Find a study buddy.*

Some people who start running find it helpful to run with a partner. It's a lot easier to blow off your daily run when the only person it affects is you. It's much harder to skip a day when your running partner comes knocking on your door. Unfortunately, finding someone who wants to study the same language may be difficult. And if one of you already has some knowledge of the language, this can make the less knowledgeable partner feel like they're behind. If you're taking a course, you might be able to partner with a classmate of similar ability. You also might be able to find a study partner online.

4. *Study at the same time each day.*

Most of us have a preferred time of day for accomplishing important tasks. Some find the quiet of early morning to be best for study and writing, while others are night owls, and do their best work late in the day. As an adult language learner, you probably have a good sense of what works best for you. Studying every morning before or after breakfast, or late at night, before a midnight snack, might be options to consider. If you're consistent about this, then the time of day will serve as a trigger and reminder for your study.

## A Sense of Self

As you consider your goal of learning a foreign language, there are many factors you need to keep in mind: your motivation, how much time you'll have for study, and whether or not to take formal classes in your target language. You'll wonder whether you're too old for such an undertaking (you're not!). How much support will you get from friends and family? Will the effort required be worth it? How will it feel if you expend a great deal of effort, only to be dissatisfied with your level of fluency? Only you can answer some of these questions, but it may be helpful to consider some concepts from social psychology that are relevant to these issues.

The term *self-efficacy* was coined by Albert Bandura in the early 1970s to refer to a person's belief in her ability to accomplish something: to perform a task, reach a goal, or overcome an obstacle.[12] However, it's important to understand that one's self-efficacy can vary greatly from one domain to another. Perhaps you're a wizard in the kitchen: you can assemble a tasty and nutritious meal given almost any set of ingredients, you frequently watch cooking shows, and you love to try out new recipes. The self-efficacy you possess in this sphere of your life is high: you love to challenge yourself, and you derive a great deal of satisfaction from your mastery of cooking. In another sphere, however, your feelings may be decidedly different. If you're one of the many people who find internal combustion engines to be a complete mystery, you will have low self-efficacy with regard to automotive matters. You might feel helpless and depressed when your car isn't running well, and a visit to the repair shop may fill you with dread. You never understand what the mechanic is talking about, and you have no way of determining whether the bill for repairs is reasonable or not. So clearly, one's perceived level of self-efficacy can vary greatly across the different arenas of one's life.

An important thing to remember is that low self-efficacy can be a trap: it can keep even the most motivated person from trying to master things at a later point in time. Unfortunately, experiences that shape self-efficacy may happen early in life, and the memory of an unfortunate episode can last a lifetime. For example, in talking to people about the subject of this book, Richard and Roger frequently encountered negative reactions to foreign language learning. "Oh, I'm not any good at foreign languages," they might say, averting their eyes as if this were some sort of moral failing. "I studied Spanish in high school, and barely earned passing grades. The teachers made fun of my accent, and I hated studying something that I knew I would never use." So a negative experience with one language can lead to a generalized low self-efficacy with regard to learning any foreign language, in any context, and for any purpose.[13]

If you have feelings of low self-efficacy, then failing to achieve your hoped-for level of fluency might be the expected result.

Psychologists have a name for that as well: it's called a *self-fulfilling prophecy*. Because you expect a certain negative outcome, you may sabotage your efforts at mastery without even realizing it. And low self-efficacy can have a pernicious effect on your motivation, the time you spend in instruction and study, and may ultimately lead to abandoning the enterprise altogether. And this outcome will make sense to you: "I never was any good at French when I was a sophomore, so I'm not surprised that I can't learn it now."

How, then, does an adult overcome feelings of low self-efficacy in language learning that may have persisted since childhood? First of all, be sure not to confuse self-efficacy with *self-esteem*. Self-esteem refers to your overall evaluation of your worth as an individual. You can have a healthy level of self-esteem and still have feelings of low self-efficacy for certain domains (such as language learning).

Second, the best way to overcome low self-efficacy is to take practical steps to develop mastery in the desired domain. Because self-efficacy is based on doing, not being, it can be transformed through learning. The goal of this book is to help adult language learners develop a sense of self-efficacy for language learning, even if that has not been their experience in the past. Rather than think about language learning as one domain, break the different aspects of language learning into more basic units. Then start building self-efficacy by first emphasizing those aspects of language learning in which you generally do well in other domains. For example, if you know that you have a good verbal memory, then concentrate on building a large vocabulary. If you know you're a person who needs to see or hear things repeatedly before they make sense, then load up your iPhone with practice conversations. If you know you thrive on structure and organization, then create detailed diagrams as reference material. And if you're more of a free spirit, make impromptu phone calls to a fluent friend to practice your conversational skills. It doesn't matter what you do to get started, as long as you do what you're good at. As you continue to improve, your self-efficacy will grow. As an adult language learner, you have the gift of insight—something younger learners lack. Don't be afraid to take advantage of it.

### Trying Hard Not to Try Hard

Martina Navratilova was a force of nature in the tennis world throughout the 1970s and '80s. She won dozens of singles and doubles titles, and was clearly one of the strongest and most consistent players of her generation. One of the cruel realities of the sporting world, however, is that you can't stay on top forever. By the late 1980s, Navratilova had passed the age of thirty, and younger players were beginning to threaten her. At the French Open in 1987, she lost to the eighteen-year old Steffi Graf. In the same year, she was beaten by the sixteen-year old Gabriela Sabatini in the Italian Open. When interviewed about these defeats, Navratilova's response was revealing. She said:

I was afraid to play my best. I felt so threatened by those young kids coming up, Graf particularly, wondering whether they were better than me ... I daren't give those matches 100 per cent.

The idea that a world-class tennis player would intentionally undercut her own performance may seem quite strange. Why on earth would she do this, particularly against opponents who would seem to require all of her skill? Navratilova herself provided the answer in the very next sentence of the interview:

I was scared to find out if they could beat me when I'm playing my best because, if they can, then I am finished.

Welcome to the world of inverted logic known as *self-handicapping*.[14] And it's not just tennis stars or other athletes who fall prey to this destructive behavior. Self-handicapping is doubly harmful because since it leads to failure, and neatly provides a ready-made excuse for that failure.

Imagine a college student who has an important exam the following day. The test is in a course he's been having problems with, and he's not sure how well he will do. Nevertheless, he spends the night before drinking with his frat brothers instead of studying. Paradoxically, this student now has all of his bases covered. If he does poorly on the test the following day, he can make what researchers call a *situational attribution*: "I would have done okay if I hadn't gotten drunk last night." This makes sense—everyone knows that taking a test while hungover will not truly reflect one's ability. But now imagine the other possible outcome: the student actually does well on the exam. Now his success seems even more impressive: "I got a good grade *even though* I spent the night drinking with my buddies. I must be freakin' brilliant!"

Research has shown that individuals will do almost anything to avoid a downward revision in their perceptions of themselves. And as both Navratilova and this hypothetical student demonstrate, this includes doing things that are actually quite harmful (deliberately not playing at one's best, or not studying for an exam). However, this also means that they won't perform as well as they could have. Apparently, this outcome is preferable to the one in which the student studies hard, and fails the test. And Navratilova was able to convince herself that she still could compete at the highest level of her sport, even as she allegedly allowed other, younger players to beat her.

As with self-efficacy, self-handicapping will vary depending on the context and situation. Researchers have characterized self-handicapping as either *situational* or as *chronic*. Letting your young nephew beat you at chess would be an example of the former—you don't want to crush his spirit by playing your best when he's still learning the game, and it won't keep you from trying as hard as you can to defeat your brother when you play him. However, self-handicapping can also become a way of life, as in the case of someone who persistently abuses drugs or alcohol.[15]

Keeping this discussion of self-efficacy, self-fulfilling prophecy, and self-handicapping in mind, therefore, may lessen anxiety about trying to achieve proficiency later in adulthood.[16] Don't assume that a particular outcome in the past is predictive of what can be achieved now and in the future. Capitalize on what works well, and don't let fear of failure keep you from trying your best.

**Getting in the Zone**

In your pursuit of proficiency in a foreign language, it's important that you study topics that are neither too easy nor too difficult for you at any given point in time. This is particularly true if you're studying a language largely on your own. If you already have a working knowledge of Greek, for example, it wouldn't be very helpful to spend all of your time studying basic vocabulary or completing elementary exercises, although as we will see in chapter 7, some overlearning can be beneficial. Although it may make you feel good about yourself to effortlessly rattle off simple phrases like "Where is the train station?" ultimately, rehearsing only easy material is not the best use of your study time. By the same token, if you're a beginner, then jumping into a difficult topic, like the grammar for a language's subjunctive mood, is not time well spent either.

This means that, at each point during the study of your target language, some topics and exercises will be most appropriate to your current level of expertise. Just ask Goldilocks, who found some of the bears' porridge either too hot or too cold. Like her, you are looking for topics that are "just right," given your current mastery of the material. The trick is to find this territory.

The concept we're referring to is well known in educational circles, although it has gone by different names at different times. Perhaps the first and most famous name for this concept was offered by the Russian psychologist Lev Vygotsky. In the early 1930s, he coined the term "zone of proximal development" (or ZPD) to refer to the metaphorical region between what a learner can do without help, and what a learner can do only with assistance from a guide or teacher.[17]

Educators also use other terms that have much the same flavor as the ZPD. For example, teachers and school psychologists talk about the concept of *readiness*—the cognitive state when a person will benefit from a particular educational experience. First-grade schoolchildren are not cognitively ready to study calculus, nor do they have the requisite knowledge of the mathematics that would be involved. However, they are ready to understand more concrete concepts like counting along a number line.

Sometimes, events that are unplanned or unexpected are used to foster understanding of a concept that lies within a person's ZPD. At the time we drafted this section of the book, the US news was dominated by the announcement that the city of Detroit had declared bankruptcy. Several commentators referred to this event as a *teachable moment* for understanding the economic challenges faced by large postindustrial cities in the United States. Few of us would willingly seek out arcane information about bankruptcy law, public policy, and pension obligations. However, the significance of Detroit's bankruptcy meant that millions of people were now ready to learn more about these principles of macroeconomics.

Another idea that is popular in educational circles is the concept of *scaffolding*. Just as a physical scaffold can provide support for painters and other artisans, a teacher can provide support to his or her pupils to help them master something that they can't learn on their own. And in some fields, it's assumed that once mastery is gained, it should be passed on to others as quickly as possible. Medical residents become familiar with the phrase "Watch one, do one, teach one." Doctors in their residency have to learn so many procedures that they don't have the benefit of observing, say, dozens of lumbar punctures before attempting the procedure themselves. Mastery is assumed to occur after witnessing one such operation and then a successful performance of one's own. Once a resident has successfully performed the procedure, she then can serve as the scaffold for the next doctor in training.

All of this has important implications for the adult foreign language learner. Although your neighbor down the street may be a native speaker of your target language and is willing to converse with you, he may assume that you will progress more quickly than you actually can. As you gain mastery of the foreign language, you'll begin to have a sense of your strengths and weaknesses—what's easy for you, and what typically takes you a bit more time to understand and master. You probably don't have unlimited time to study the language, so your goal should be to use your time as efficiently as possible. This means that you'll want to get in the zone—the zone of proximal development. If you find yourself completing exercises or engaging in conversations that are quite easy for you, it would be wise to increase the level of difficulty. And if your conversational partner is enthusiastically barreling along on a topic that's way over your head, it's up to you to intervene and ask to go more slowly or to provide simpler examples. Remember, just being a native speaker of a language does not make someone an effective teacher. As an adult learner you have the ability to gauge for yourself whether or not you are in the zone and make the appropriate adjustments.[18]

Think about it this way: The best way to improve your tennis game is to play against someone who is just a little bit better than you are. If you play against someone worse than you are, you'll be helping *her*—but you'll never get better yourself. If you play against someone who is much better than you, then you won't improve your game either, unless she is willing to play at a level just a little bit better than you are. Whether learning a language or playing tennis, recognizing when you are in the zone is one of the most important metacognitive skills any adult learner can develop. The ability to "think about your thinking" allows you to optimize your learning environment—on the court or in the classroom.

# 3 Aspects of Language

## *I* Before *E* / Except After *C* / or When Sounded as *A* / as in *Neighbor* or *Weigh*

When children learn language, they learn to speak before they learn to read. Some adult foreign language learners feel that they should learn their target language in much the same way. That is, they try to ignore written language until they have mastered spoken language. This misconception no doubt appears logical to speakers of English because, in English, sounds and letters do not correspond to each other in a one-to-one fashion.

The technical term for the relationship between sound and spelling is *phoneme–grapheme correspondence*. A phoneme is a sound in a language, and a grapheme is the written form for that sound. Ideally, there would be a one-to-one relationship between a sound and the letter used to represent it. English has about forty phonemes, and the Latin alphabet has only twenty-six letters, so some letters have to pull double duty. Other languages solve this problem, in part, by using *diacritics*—marks above or below letters to denote different sounds, such as *affamé* (hungry) or *façade* (front) in French. None of this would be a problem if English behaved consistently in this regard. But it doesn't.

English was frozen into type relatively early in its history, and wholesale changes in how the language was pronounced happened later. Other languages have changed more slowly than English, or have had their spelling overhauled to bring it in line with the spoken form. This didn't happen with English, and therefore, the same sound can be written in a variety of ways. Some letters are silent, but only some of the time. Exceptions abound. And it is these inconsistencies that are the bane of anyone trying to learn English as a foreign language.

The capricious nature of English spelling–sound relationships was illustrated in an example famously, but also perhaps falsely, attributed to George Bernard Shaw, the Irish playwright.[1] Consider how the word *fish* could be written as *ghoti*, given that the "f" sound can be written as "gh" in words like *enough*, that the "i" sound can be written as "o" as in *women*, and that "sh" can be written as "ti" in words like *nation*. In other words, just about anything goes. Based on "words" like *ghoti*, many people over the years have championed a wholesale reform of English spelling, and although the problem is easy to illustrate, it doesn't admit to any easy solutions.

In contrast, when Roger began studying German during his freshman year in high school, his teacher made a statement so outrageous that it has always stuck with him, "German is very regular. You'll know how to pronounce almost every word that you read, even if you've never seen it before. And you'll know how to spell almost every word that you hear." This seemed like an utter impossibility—and it is, if your frame of reference is English.

If we think about a language's spelling and sound consistency as points on a continuum, with one endpoint denoting perfect consistency and the other denoting perfect chaos, then English could be thought of as the "Wild West." Many languages, however, do show impressive levels of spelling and sound consistency. Finnish, Greek, the syllabary systems of Japanese, and Spanish all fare well in this regard. The spelling–sound correspondences are regular, and exceptions are few (and mostly involve foreign terms borrowed from other languages). And at other points along this spelling–sound continuum, we would find languages like Arabic, French, and Hebrew—languages that are more regular than English, but less consistent than the ideal.

There are real-world consequences to a lack of correspondence between spellings and sound. Developmental studies have shown that children have more difficulty in decoding words in inconsistent languages, like English, and learn to read more slowly as a result. And as mentioned earlier, adult speakers of other languages attempting to learn English find these inconsistencies bizarre and frustrating. Nevertheless, these difficulties do not cause English speakers to stop reading or writing. And they make spelling bees possible, which aren't needed in languages like Spanish, which have a regular phoneme–grapheme correspondence.

Given this state of affairs, it's no wonder that people are advised to focus solely on speaking and listening so as not to be confused by the irregularities that might be found in reading and writing a foreign language.[2] However, the educational psychologist David Ausubel pointed out two reasons why written and spoken materials should be presented in tandem. First, he noted that by adolescence, the vast majority of adults are already quite proficient at learning new information through a combination of reading and listening. Consequently, it would be unnatural *not* to learn new material that way. Therefore, to focus only on spoken material "deprives the older learner of his principal learning tool and of the instructional medium in which he feels most comfortable and confident. This is particularly unfortunate during the early phases of instruction when learning stresses tend to be the greatest."[3]

Second, Ausubel pointed out that reading can be an invaluable support for spoken language. Especially early on in the acquisition of a new language, unfamiliar sounds and sound combinations, stress patterns, word boundaries, and grammatical structures are difficult to differentiate. Providing written materials in conjunction with spoken materials gives adult language learners additional cues with which they can make these distinctions. As students learn to speak and read concurrently, these materials can be alternated, or gradually withdrawn, when the time comes to strengthen purely spoken or purely written modes of communication.

As you learn a new language, therefore, be sure to learn to both read and speak the language at the same time. It may seem like slow going at first (depending on the language you are learning) but at least if you are a native speaker of English, it is likely that you will find more consistency in your target language than in your native tongue. Not only will you be as amazed as Roger was to learn that spelling and sound can indeed coexist harmoniously, but you will also be reinforcing your speaking and listening through reading, and vice versa. You are already an adult who knows how to do both—why try to learn a language by denying yourself one of your obvious strengths?

## Behind the Scenes at the Foreign Service Institute

It is only natural to compare ourselves to others. Doing so provides valuable feedback about progress. But it is important to make the proper comparisons in order to put language learning in perspective. Therefore, before thinking about your own language progress, consider the gold standard of foreign language learning: the Foreign Service Institute (FSI).

The Foreign Service Institute is the US Department of State's training center for diplomats and other individuals who work for the US government in the field of foreign affairs. FSI has branches in various parts of the world, but the largest by far is the George P. Shultz National Foreign Affairs Training Center (NFATC) located in Arlington, Virginia, just outside Washington, DC. Each year more than 100,000 students enroll in over 700 courses at NFATC. These courses are designed to prepare Foreign Service Officers and others for their work advancing US interests at the more than 290 embassies, consulates, and other types of diplomatic missions around the world. Organized much like a university, FSI offers traditional classroom and online courses in a wide range of areas, including leadership, crisis management, diplomatic tradecraft, information technology, and safety and security.

The Foreign Service Institute is most famous, however, for its School of Language Studies. More than seventy languages are taught at FSI (although not all are being taught at any given time). But not everyone who works at a diplomatic mission abroad receives language training. In general, language classes are provided only to those individuals serving in language designated positions (LDPs). Furthermore, not everyone going into an LDP receives the same amount of instruction. FSI measures language proficiency on the Interagency Language Roundtable (ILR) scale, which describes levels of proficiency that range from 0 (no proficiency) to 5 (functionally native proficiency). Although there are several different types of proficiency (i.e., speaking, reading, listening, writing, translation performance, interpretation performance, competence in intercultural communication, and audio translation performance), LDPs are only specified for speaking (S) and reading (R). There are approximately 4,100 language designated positions worldwide, the majority of which require speaking and reading scores of 3 (general professional proficiency) which is notated as S3/R3, or called just "3-3" for short. We discuss these levels in more detail in the next section on measuring proficiency.

As you can imagine, not everyone who will serve in an S3/R3 language designated position will study their target language for the same amount of time. The length of time designated to reach S3/R3 in any given language depends on the difficulty of the target language. Difficulty is determined by how long it should take a native speaker of English to go from no proficiency (0) to general professional proficiency (3). Diplomats studying languages such as Spanish, Italian, Portuguese, Swedish, and Dutch are expected to reach S3/R3 proficiency in 24 weeks. French takes 30 weeks. Students who need to speak languages such as German, Indonesian, and Swahili receive 36 weeks of training. Languages at the next highest level of difficulty, so-called "hard" languages, such as Russian, Urdu, and Burmese, require 44 weeks of training. Finally, to get to an S3/R3 with no prior background in the so-called "super hard" languages of Arabic, Chinese (Mandarin and Cantonese), Japanese, and Korean takes almost two years (88 weeks).

Of course, these times are only averages established by FSI based on the success rates of previous students; they are reviewed periodically and subject to change. The reason some languages are expected to take longer to master than others is complex. But in general, the more closely the language is related to English, the more quickly the language can be mastered. For example, French is more closely related to English than Thai; therefore, for an English speaker, Thai is expected to take longer than French. Likewise, Spanish uses a writing system similar to that of English, but Arabic does not. Therefore, students are expected to spend less time studying Spanish than Arabic. Other factors, too, influence the perceived level of difficulty, such as how similar the sound system of the language is to English, but you get the point.

Because FSI is a government-funded entity, it is also evaluated periodically by the Office of the Inspector General (OIG). In fiscal year (FY) 2012, the OIG reported that the success rate for students with no prior knowledge of a target language reaching a designated S3/R3 level was 60 percent. However, since most students who do not attain their desired score in the allotted time period continue to study, the overall success rate ultimately rises to 82 percent. Interestingly, two of the languages with the lowest on-time success rates were not Arabic or Chinese, but rather French and German.[4]

One thing to keep in mind is that for the vast majority of language students studying at FSI, learning the target language is their full-time job. These students receive four or five hours a day of direct language instruction in classes of no more than four students, with many receiving one-to-one instruction. Because studying their target language is their full-time job, students at FSI are expected to be on campus for at least eight hours a day, using the time outside of language class for self-study. FSI also provides state-of-the-art language laboratories, a library with language learning and reference materials, and Internet-enabled classrooms. Is it any wonder, therefore, that most of these students eventually reach their language goals?

Whether you are a student at FSI preparing for your assignment in Tirana, or a working parent who always wanted to learn Italian, don't worry about whether the language is easy, hard, or super hard. In the end, the perceived difficulty of the language matters far less than your attachment to the language. If you are fascinated by China, study Chinese, and remember to cut yourself some slack if you aren't memorizing vocabulary words as easily as your friend who is studying Spanish. And also remember that 40 percent of students at FSI, with all of the resources available to them, don't reach the designated S3/R3 in the estimated time, but they don't give up—and neither should you.

### Measuring Fluency and Proficiency

Most people use the term *fluency* to mean how well a person speaks a foreign language. In fact, we used the term that way in the title of this book. However, linguists, educators, speech pathologists, and others define fluency more specifically, and each slightly differently, depending on their goals.[5] Technically, fluency depends on rate of speech. In other words, a person is fluent in a language if he speaks it rapidly, smoothly, and accurately. The term fluency in this sense is different from *proficiency*, which refers to one's competence using the language. If this seems like splitting hairs, consider the following.

*Aphasia* is a general term for loss of language after brain injury.[6] One type of aphasia, called *nonfluent* or *Broca's* aphasia, is characterized by halting, effortful, and yet still meaningful speech. People with Broca's aphasia cannot express themselves fluently; nonetheless, because they still possess knowledge of the language and are able to make themselves understood, they can be said to have retained linguistic proficiency after the brain injury. In contrast, people with *fluent* or *Wernicke's* aphasia speak rapidly and effortlessly, but make little sense.

Here is another example. An opera singer who has memorized the score of a libretto can sing the opera perfectly and expressively, and yet be unable to leave the opera house and hail a taxi using that language. The singer could be said to be demonstrating fluency, and yet not be proficient in the language. Likewise, a poorly educated native speaker of a language could be considered fluent, but without having attained a high level of proficiency.

But the distinction between fluency and proficiency doesn't really matter for most adult foreign language learners. Because being fluent in a language is generally understood to imply a high level of proficiency, most foreign language learners are working toward both goals.

It's not easy to quantify how well someone speaks a foreign language. One person may boast that he is 100 percent fluent, but be unable to order a meal in a restaurant. Another person may apologize for her poor linguistic ability as she uses the target language to deconstruct Kierkegaard's use of irony. One way to solve this problem would be to create a scale that objectively measures linguistic ability, and, as introduced in the previous section, this is exactly what FSI did. Let's take a look at this scale in more detail and see how it applies to the adult foreign language learner.

As noted earlier, proficiency on the ILR scale can be assigned a score from 0 to 5. A score of 0 is equivalent to no proficiency in a language. Richard and Roger both have a S0/R0 in Hindi, because neither one of them can speak or read Hindi. At the other end of the scale, people who receive the highest score of 5 demonstrate a functionally native proficiency. For example, a score of S5 means that someone speaks a target language like a highly educated, articulate, native speaker. As odd as it may seem, not all native speakers of a language speak or read their own language at level 5. If you'd like to learn more about the ILR scale, or if you'd like to take a self-assessment for speaking, reading or listening, go to http://govtilr.org/.

Let's look in depth at Levels 1 through 4 of the ILR Speaking Skill Scale with regard to the area of speaking, since most adult language learners concentrate on speaking when they study a foreign language

Level 1: Elementary Proficiency

Speakers of a language at Level 1 can introduce themselves (name, age, country of origin) and can engage in simple, predictable conversations. They can usually exchange greetings and follow politeness rules. Native speakers must speak slowly and clearly to them, often repeating what they've said in order to be understood. Likewise, the native speaker must work hard to understand what is being said by a Level 1 speaker. The Level 1 speaker may often be misunderstood, and his vocabulary is limited and might be inaccurate. He makes some errors in basic grammar and pronunciation. A Level 1 speaker may be someone who took the language as an elective in high school and/or college, and can speak the language in an elementary way.

Speaking a language at Level 1 is an appropriate goal for many adult language learners. S1 ability demonstrates that you took the time and effort to study someone else's language and will win you many points among native speakers. It takes hard work to get to Level 1. Don't focus on what you can't do, focus on all that you can.

Level 2: Limited Working Proficiency

People who speak a language at Level 2 can easily satisfy the demands of everyday social situations and can fulfill basic work requirements. However, they still have difficulty with complex tasks. They can engage in everyday conversations on basic topics (e.g., the weather, current events, work, and family). They have trouble, however, when conversations veer from routine topics. The Level 2 speaker won't make mistakes with basic grammar and vocabulary, but his utterances are still not very sophisticated. He may try to overextend his limited vocabulary. For example, rather than differentiate between *beautiful*, *gorgeous*, *stunning*, *attractive*, or *cute*, he uses the word *pretty* in every situation. The use of complex grammatical structures (for example, the subjunctive in certain languages) is still weak or nonexistent. A person who majors in a language in college could be expected to speak that language at Level 2 upon graduation.

Adult language learners who reach Level 2 can be justifiably proud of this accomplishment. With Level 2 abilities, adults can get around quite easily using the target language. The confidence that comes from speaking at Level 2 is very freeing, because one need not rely on native speakers to fulfill basic needs. Speaking at Level 2 often propels people to work even harder to achieve Level 3 proficiency.

Level 3: General Professional Proficiency

The grammar and vocabulary of a speaker at Level 3 is sufficient to participate in most formal and informal conversations. She will use the language well, but there are still some noticeable limitations. She can speak at a normal rate, and native speakers do not need to slow down to speak to her. The Level 3 speaker may still have some difficulty, however, with figurative language (e.g., metaphors, idiomatic expressions, and proverbs) or cultural references. Also, her accent still sounds somewhat foreign. A Level 3 speaker easily understands, and is easily understood by native speakers. This is the level to which most adult language learners strive. A person with a master's degree in a language probably speaks the language at Level 3. If the definition of fluency is being able to express oneself readily and effortlessly, then Level 3 speakers can say that they are fluent in a language.

Level 4: Advanced Professional Proficiency

A Level 4 speaker makes few speech errors. The Level 4 speaker uses cultural references and figures of speech appropriately. For example, a Level 4 speaker may accurately use sarcasm. These speakers may also be able to act as nonprofessional interpreters between the target language and their native language. The Level 4 speaker also understands various dialects of the language. Level 4 speakers differ from Level 5 speakers only in subtle ways, occasionally saying something in a way that a native speaker would not.

As you think about these levels, keep in mind that an ILR score will not reflect a person's ability to live in or adjust to another culture. The real test of how well you speak a language is how easily you communicate when you are using that language, and the pleasure you derive from speaking it. The important point is to think about exactly what you want to accomplish with your language study, and to work in that direction. Do you want to speak formally for work or do you want to just make friends? Keep in mind that proficiency is a continuum, with different levels and areas and ways to measure them. So, go at your own pace and emphasize your strengths. Test scores can be useful, but they can also cause you to forget what it is you want to accomplish with the language. And as you are studying, when you get frustrated or feel like giving up, just remember that native speakers don't speak their native language perfectly either; rather, they speak it well enough to accomplish their communicative goals. Why hold yourself to a higher standard?

## Interlanguage

In a humorous essay in the *New York Times*, Philip Crawford recounts how he once said "Bon appétit" to his French wife and son before a meal and was roundly chastised for being gauche.[7] He appealed to French friends who were professors and they basically agreed with his family, although they acknowledged that "the subject is indeed delicate and would deserve a symposium involving linguists, socio-linguistics, teachers of good manners, specialists of customs and traditions, plus a few duchesses." It should be noted that Mr. Crawford was living in France and had studied French for over thirty years when he committed this faux pas.

Perhaps you too have been surprised that, once you achieved a level of fluency in a language where you got around quite comfortably, you discovered that a word or phrase you had been using consistently for a long period of time was, in fact, wrong. And like Mr. Crawford at the dinner table, perhaps you felt so sure you were right that you found yourself trying to correct a native speaker! How does this happen?

As individuals learn a language, they are gradually acquiring new sounds, vocabulary words, grammatical structures, and ways to use the language socially. With regard to the ILR scale, any language ability between 0 and 5 can be considered an *interlanguage*.[8] In other words, your interlanguage is how you speak a particular language between the time you start studying that language and the point at which you have achieved complete mastery. Most adult language learners, therefore, will be contending with an interlanguage for many years.

Although a person's interlanguage is specific to that individual, and because it comprises that speaker's own unique set of learned (and unlearned) material, all adult language learners do similar things with their interlanguage. First, out of necessity, they draw upon their native language to learn the new language. Depending on the two languages, sometimes this language transfer is helpful, as in true cognates between languages, and sometimes it interferes, as in using English word order in Japanese. Second, once a person learns a new word or grammatical structure, he will tend to overgeneralize. That is, he will use this new word or structure a lot—and sometimes in ways that are not appropriate. For example, one of the first words English speakers studying Korean learn is a word that means *complicated*. They learn this word early on because it sounds a lot like the English word "pork chop." Because it is such an easy word to learn, suddenly everything that has any level of complexity at all becomes "pork chop" even when it's not appropriate, such as to describe a traffic jam or a difficult test question. But unless the speaker knows how to say *traffic congestion* or *tricky question*, "pork chop" is all one has to work with.

This overgeneralization makes sense because if you have a vocabulary of only a few hundred words, chances are you will be forced to try to extend their usage. In fact, overgeneralization and language transfer can occur together, since you try to use a learned vocabulary word in all of the same ways you can use a word with the same meaning in your native language. Finally, because a person's interlanguage is less than optimal, it is by definition a simplified version of the language.

Obviously, therefore, some of the things you say in your interlanguage will be correct and some will be incorrect. But the mistakes will be unique to you because—as mistakes—these are presumably not utterances you've ever heard from a native speaker. Ideally, as you keep learning a language, the number of correct utterances will grow and the number of incorrect utterances will decline, which means that theoretically your interlanguage should progress systematically toward mastery in an orderly way.

Unfortunately, it doesn't work that way. Interlanguages are not orderly. There is great variability among speakers—even those studying together in the same class. Furthermore, improvement in one's interlanguage may stop or greatly slow down, which is referred to as *fossilization*.[9] Once you reach a point where you are able to do most of the things you want in a language, you no longer have the need to keep improving. Because you are generally intelligible, native speakers may stop correcting minor errors, as long as they do not interfere with intelligibility. This may lead you to stop expecting their feedback, causing you to believe that you have achieved a certain level of mastery, when in fact you have not. If you reach this point, not only will your linguistic skill improve much more slowly, but you may also find yourself going backward, making mistakes in areas that you had previously mastered.

When and how fossilization happens depends on many factors, one of which will be your motivation to learn the language. At a certain point, you may feel that you speak the language well enough so that further instruction is not worth the additional effort. You may recognize that there is still much you don't know, but what you do know is sufficient to your purpose and therefore you stop pushing yourself.

In addition, your interlanguage can become fossilized in more subtle ways. Because the people around you have become used to your speech habits, they may speak to you like you speak to them—even though they know it is not exactly right. Perhaps you are guilty of this as well. Have you ever found yourself speaking less than perfect English to a nonnative speaker? Don't be surprised, then, when a native speaker in your target language does the same thing to you. This is yet another reason why one's interlanguage can become prematurely fossilized with minor, and perhaps not so minor, errors.

**I Know You Know What I Know**

Although teachers generally avoid the habit of not correcting even minor errors, they do become familiar with your particular way of speaking. Your teacher knows your accent, knows the vocabulary you have mastered, knows the grammatical structures you use most frequently, and knows the topics you like to discuss. All of this means that your teacher is likely to understand you far better than native speakers who don't know you.

Among diplomats who study foreign languages at FSI, this phenomenon is known as "FSI Speak." You too may have found yourself being understood in the classroom with teachers and classmates, while outside the classroom your efforts fell flat. Why is there sometimes a sharp distinction between what one can do with the language in class and what one can do with the language in the real world? An answer can be found by considering what cognitive scientists call *common ground*.[10]

Keeping track of common ground is not specific to foreign language learning. All speakers take into consideration which personal and situational factors are shared, and which are not shared, by their conversational partners. In other words, when speaking to someone, you must take into account what you know they know and what you know they don't know. Now consider how much more of a problem monitoring common ground will be when speaking with someone whose culture you don't share, and whose language you are still learning. It's hardly surprising, therefore, that you will be more fluent with your teacher and classmates than with a cab driver. Unfortunately, adult language learners sometimes attribute this discrepancy in fluency to their own lack of language-learning ability, or they may blame their teachers for not preparing them appropriately for real-world interactions with native speakers.

One way to improve your chances of being understood outside the classroom, therefore, is to think about what the other person might share with you, and then to enlarge upon this common ground by filling in missing information. For example, you might start by using greetings and pleasantries to establish how you speak the language, which will help your conversational partner get used to your accent. In addition, you may want to ask your conversational partner questions that will also help establish more familiarity. Keep in mind that even though you do this automatically in your native language, it's easy to lose track of common ground when you are trying to communicate in a relatively unfamiliar foreign language. Moreover, just being aware that you will likely speak the target language better with people you know than with strangers should reduce your frustration in these situations.

It is also possible that the way you speak the language could signify differences in common ground that are not really there. These kinds of mismatches can create confusion, hurt feelings, and misunderstandings. For example, when Richard studied

French at FSI, he learned mainly the polite *vous* form of verbs—which is what he needed to use at work. At one point, however, a friend he'd made in Niger said that his continued use of the formal *vous* instead of the informal *tu* made him feel that Richard was maintaining a wall between them. Richard, however, did not know the *tu* form of verbs very well, so he was forced to use *vous*. Although using *vous* made Richard sound professional at work, he was unaware that he came across as cold and distant in everyday situations. His teachers at FSI would have understood, but how could anyone else be expected to? To correct the situation, Richard expanded the shared common ground with his friend by explaining how he had learned only professional French. He next worked harder on learning the *tu* form of verbs.

In summary, it may seem obvious, but it is crucial nevertheless, to recognize that unless you have complete mastery of a language, you have only partial competence. To keep your interlanguage from becoming fossilized, it is important to become neither complacent nor frustrated when you plateau at a particular level. Remember too that in your native language, you make linguistic choices that reflect the common ground you believe you share with others. A problem arises, however, when native speakers assume that you are choosing from among the full range of linguistic possibilities available in the target language, when in fact your ability to express yourself is limited by what you have and have not learned. Your conversational partner, being unaware of what you don't know, may misinterpret your intentions.

To improve overall fluency, therefore, it is important to engage as many different speakers of your target language in as many different contexts as possible. It's also important to push your conversational partners to correct you and give you suggestions.

As long as you are being understood, they may avoid doing so out of politeness, so it is important to tell them that you want to be corrected. Moreover, don't be defensive when a teacher or other well-meaning person points out to you that what you meant is not what you said—even if you've said it that way a thousand times before. As irritating as this is, being open to it will keep your interlanguage from becoming fossilized and will help you establish the common ground you need for successful communication.

# 4  Pragmatics and Culture

## The Language, the Culture, and You

Throughout this book, we repeatedly point out that adult language learners possess advantages over younger language learners—the most important of which is their ability to reflect on their own language learning process. Nowhere is this metalinguistic ability more apparent, and more useful, than in the study of *pragmatics*, which is the social use of language. In this chapter we will examine how cognitive scientists have studied pragmatics. Unfortunately, this topic is often ignored in traditional foreign language learning settings. Therefore, it is important to set the scene with some background information before going on to discuss how pragmatics applies to learning a foreign language. To do this, we must think about language at a *metalinguistic* level.

Because pragmatics is the social use of language, it lends itself quite easily to metalinguistic awareness. In contrast, one's metalinguistic ability to reflect on the sound system of a language is limited. Young children cannot take a mental step back and think metalinguistically about the sound system of the language(s) they are learning. They also don't need to do this because they possess the skill of distinguishing, and then later producing, sounds just by hearing them. Even though adult language learners can (and in fact must) consciously think about the sound distinctions between their native language and the target language, doing so never entirely makes up for the fact that sounds not learned in childhood are more difficult to distinguish and produce in adulthood. In other words, just reflecting on the sounds of a language cannot completely compensate for the advantages of early exposure.

Metalinguistic skill is more useful when it comes to learning vocabulary and grammar. In these two areas, research has shown that adults are not necessarily at a disadvantage when compared to children.[1] For adult language learners, metacognitive skills can be effectively employed so that words and the rules for combining them can be more easily learned, retained, and retrieved. But as important as metacognitive skills are for learning the vocabulary and grammar of a language, in these areas they only serve as a means to an end. In fact, the goal for using metacognitive skills in language learning is to eventually stop relying on these skills. That is to say, once we have mastered certain words, phrases, or grammatical patterns, we no longer have a reason to consciously reflect on them. In fact, continuing to do so would be counterproductive and would slow down the flow of communication.

Pragmatics, however, is the one linguistic domain where adult language learners continue to leverage their metalinguistic and metacognitive strengths, even after full mastery of a language is achieved. Even native speakers, who automatically produce sounds, words, and phrases, still must consciously reflect on what they say to maximize its effectiveness. Therefore, as the linguistic domain in which adult language learners most excel, we place special emphasis on the importance of pragmatics. We believe that an understanding of pragmatics not only can help the adult learner acquire a new language, but will also help him or her continue to use this language to the fullest.

The successful use of pragmatics requires a deep knowledge of the culture in which the target language is embedded. Not surprisingly, therefore, pragmatic ability is often considered the most advanced aspect of linguistic mastery. For example, according to the ILR Skill Level descriptions, it is only when speakers reach the S-4 (advanced professional proficiency) level that they are expected to "organize discourse well, employing functional rhetorical speech devices, native cultural references, and understanding." Furthermore, it is not until the S-5 (native or bilingual proficiency) level that speakers are expected to use the language "with complete flexibility and intuition, so that speech on all levels is fully accepted by well-educated native speakers in all of its features, including breadth of vocabulary and idioms, colloquialisms, and pertinent cultural references."[2]

We do not disagree with the ILR classifications. Clearly an *inability* "to use speech on all levels that are fully accepted by well-educated native speakers" would mean that a language learner has not reached S-5 proficiency. We are concerned, however, that important pragmatic aspects of linguistic competence, such as the use of rhetorical speech devices, might be considered too advanced for beginning adult language learners to tackle, thereby putting off the study of these important aspects of the language. This would be a mistake. Delaying pragmatics until pronunciation, vocabulary, and grammar are well in hand deprives adult language learners of the richness and subtlety that makes learning a new language such a pleasure. It also misses ways in which pragmatics can reinforce those very skills.

There are three reasons why pragmatics should be included in language study from the very beginning of foreign language learning. First, layering pragmatics into even very basic language lessons gives the adult learner more opportunities to strengthen pronunciation, vocabulary, and grammar. Second, because it is culturally dependent, the study of pragmatics helps students better understand the culture, which will result in using the language more effectively. Finally, through pragmatics, speakers are able to convey complex meanings naturally and efficiently, which keeps them more fully engaged in their language learning.

**Cooperation**

Regardless of the target language, there is one pragmatic principle from which all spoken and written communication derives: cooperation. The philosopher of language H. Paul Grice famously described the primacy of cooperation as a conversational imperative in his "Cooperative Principle," which states: "Make your conversational contribution such as is required, at the stage at which it occurs, by the accepted purpose or direction of the talk exchange in which you are engaged."[3] In theory, for a conversation to succeed, both conversational participants must try to communicate as effectively and efficiently as possible. But what happens when one of the conversational partners is a nonnative speaker of the language? Grice's framework can help answer that question.

Grice proposed several rules, which he called "maxims," that speakers and listeners follow in order to cooperate fully. The first maxim is called the Maxim of Quantity. This maxim states that when you speak, you should not give any more information or any less information than is truly needed to make yourself understood. To give more or less information is to be uncooperative. The second maxim, the Maxim of Quality, states that you should tell the truth. To be less than truthful, therefore, is also to be uncooperative. The third maxim, the Maxim of Relation, is very straightforward: It means, "Be relevant." And finally, Grice jokingly defined the fourth Maxim of Manner as "be perspicuous," by which he meant, be clear, avoid being ambiguous, and be orderly.

Unfortunately, in many formalized language learning situations, adhering to these four maxims is all that is asked of teacher and student: Be precise, be clear, be direct, be relevant. But in natural language, as you may have guessed, speaking this way is the exception rather than the rule. People often say too much, or too little, aren't relevant, or are purposefully vague or indirect. Grice called this "flouting" the maxims. Importantly, when a maxim is flouted, the conversation doesn't automatically break down for two native speakers of a language. Conversational robustness is maintained because of the underlying assumption of cooperation. Consequently, when a speaker flouts a maxim by saying too much or too little, or is indirect, untruthful, or vague, rather than give up in frustration, the listener tries to figure out just why the speaker chose to speak that way.

For example, consider possible answers to the question "Do you like my tie?" Strictly adhering to the Cooperative Principle would produce answers like "Yes, I like your tie" or "No, I do not like your tie." These are the kinds of straightforward answers that might be expected in a typical language-learning setting.

But what about the answer "It certainly matches your shirt." This response is not entirely relevant because it does not answer the question directly. But, if both participants assume each is trying to cooperate, then, although not entirely relevant, the response not only answers the question, but does so in an inoffensive, humorous way. Therefore, by flouting the Maxim of

Relation the speaker was able to accomplish much more than merely answering the question with a "yes" or "no." Notice, however, that by answering in this way, the speaker also ran the risk of being misunderstood.

Here is another example, this time violating the Maxim of Quality. On a very stormy day, you meet a friend on the street who is soaked through with rain and you say, "Lovely weather we're having." Clearly you are not being truthful—but your friend may laugh or groan and agree with you. In this case, your friend doesn't call you a liar—your friend recognizes your greeting for what it is—sarcasm. In other words, not only is the speaker saying that the weather is bad, the speaker is also trying to be funny while at the same time seeking commiseration. Nevertheless, once again it must be pointed out that by answering sarcastically, the speaker could have been misunderstood.

Are there times when we no longer assume a conversational partner is cooperating? Yes. For example, if someone is schizophrenic, the listener may come to the conclusion that the person is incapable of cooperating and therefore no longer works to make sense of what is being said.[4] Alternatively, in a court of law, since a hostile witness cannot be assumed to be cooperating, the questioning of such a witness must use different tactics. Conversational cooperation may also be lacking in an argument between two people, where each may feign ignorance, lie, misconstrue statements, or use any means possible to win. But the fact that such examples are relatively rare indicates that conversational cooperation is the norm.

Unfortunately, most foreign language learning environments do not teach students how to flout conversational maxims in ways that are appropriate for the target language and culture. This means that foreign language learners may find themselves

stuck in an artificial world of complete and total cooperation—
which is as dull as it is unnatural. Or they may try to flout the
maxims inappropriately. That is why it is important for adult
language learners to learn how to flout these maxims for a specific culture. Although it is possible for nonnative speakers to be
misunderstood when they try to flout conversational maxims,
the underlying assumption of cooperation is robust enough to
keep the conversation flowing without too much difficulty. In
other words, there is much to be gained by being just a little bit
uncooperative.

## Speech Act Theory

For the underlying assumption of cooperation to convey more
than a mere statement of fact, all spoken and written communication must be analyzed at three different linguistic levels.
Taken together, these three levels tell us "How to Do Things with
Words," which was the title of a collection of posthumously
published lectures the philosopher of language J. L. Austin deliv-
ered at Harvard in 1955. These lectures form the core of an area
of pragmatics known as speech act theory.[5]

Consider the following situation. You are drinking a cup of
coffee at Starbucks minding your own business when a stranger
approaches you and asks, "Come here often?" You reply "Drop
dead." At a basic, literal level, "drop dead" is a statement in
which you command the person to die suddenly. Such a statement at its most literal level is called a *locutionary act* in speech
act theory. But in this case, "drop dead" is not meant literally.
What you are really doing is telling the person not to bother
you. Thus the nonliteral interpretation of your utterance (or
the *illocutionary force* of your utterance) means "go away" rather

than "die." Understanding the illocutionary force requires the cooperation of the listener to move past the literal meaning to the nonliteral meaning (also called the *figurative* meaning). Finally, what speech act theory calls the *perlocutionary effect* of the utterance—the action or state of mind brought about by that utterance—will depend on what happens next. If your would-be masher goes away, then leaving becomes the perlocutionary effect of having said "drop dead." If the person laughs and sits down next to you, then this becomes the perlocutionary effect.

Notice that speech act theory does not guarantee a specific perlocutionary outcome based on a particular speech act. Instead, speech act theory serves to remind us that for each utterance, a listener must reflect on what was said literally, figuratively, and also the outcome. For some speech acts, these three levels are all very similar. A statement such as "The sky is blue" may literally be a statement of fact, have no separate figurative meaning, and elicit no effect other than agreement by the listener. A question such as "Is the sky blue?" however, although literally a question about the color of the sky, can figuratively be used as a rhetorical question deriding someone for stating the obvious. Hopefully the speaker gauged correctly and the result was laughter and not a bloody nose.

### Figurative Language

Both Grice's Cooperative Principle and speech act theory illustrate how speakers and listeners have choices when they communicate—only one of which is to speak literally. Unfortunately, because literal language is sufficient to convey meaning, nonliteral, figurative language is often ignored in traditional language learning situations. When figurative language is taught at all, it is seen only as an interesting aside or a fun component to a lesson, which implies that it is not a necessary or integral part of language learning. Not until students are well on their way to mastering pronunciation, vocabulary and grammar does explicitly teaching figurative language begin in earnest. And perhaps there is some logic in this. Which is more important linguistically, to be able to say that a piece of pie is delicious or to say that it's a little slice of heaven? However, such a narrow view that literal language should be taught before figurative language ignores research in the area of pragmatics, which has shown that figurative speech is as fundamental to a language as its literal counterpart.[6]

The bias toward literal language in traditional language learning situations may also occur because literal language is meant to be less ambiguous than figurative language. For example, it's more straightforward to state "I'm hot" than it is to complain "I'm melting" (unless you are the Wicked Witch of the West, in which case she's speaking literally). In this way, individuals who use figurative language run a greater risk of being misunderstood than those who adhere to the strictly literal. However, as we noted earlier, if Grice is correct in that conversational participants try to express themselves as clearly as possible, you might expect potentially ambiguous figurative language to be rare. This is not the case. It's hard to imagine any language that does not use figures of speech. A fundamental example involving metaphor would be the English verb *to be*, which comes from the same root as the Sanskrit for *to breathe*.[7] That's as basic as it gets.

Figurative language is so common, therefore, that it must be the case that despite its potential ambiguity, it can accomplish discourse goals literal language cannot. In other words, although producers of figurative language run the risk of being misunderstood, there are also substantial benefits that make it worth the risk. Because specific figures of speech and the goals that they accomplish differ from language to language, it is up to you to explore these issues in your target language. To understand the concepts, let's look at some examples of figurative language in English.

It has not been clearly established exactly how many different figures of speech there are—estimates range into the hundreds. Common figures of speech that have been researched by cognitive scientists, however, include hyperbole (or exaggeration), understatement, irony, metaphor, simile, idiomatic expressions, indirect requests, and rhetorical questions. These eight figures of speech can be found throughout the world's languages; however, their use may differ from culture to culture, even for those who speak the same language. For example, for a long time Americans have been seen as greatly prone to exaggeration whereas the British are considered to be the masters of understatement. Queen Elizabeth II famously described a particularly bad year in her life this way: "1992 is not a year on which I shall look back with undiluted pleasure."[8] Likewise, some cultures value indirectness (e.g., Japan and Korea), whereas others are considered to be more direct (e.g., the United States). As you can see, figurative language is the Swiss Army knife of communication.

In a paper entitled "Why Do People Use Figurative Language?" we reported many reasons why English speakers use different figures of speech (see table 4.1). This table shows that speakers who use figurative language can do much more with their speech than those who merely stick to literal statements.

Although these data are only specific to English, the point here is that it is imperative to learn about figurative language from the very beginning of any language study. Although

**Table 4.1**
Discourse goal taxonomy

| Discourse goal | Hyperbole | Understatement | Irony | Metaphor | Simile | Idioms | Indirect requests | Rhetorical questions |
|---|---|---|---|---|---|---|---|---|
| To be conventional | | | | | | ✓ | | |
| To be eloquent | | | | ✓ | | | | |
| To be humorous | ✓ | | ✓ | ✓ | ✓ | ✓ | | |
| To protect the self | | | | | | | ✓ | |
| To compare similarities | | | | ✓ | ✓ | | | |
| To emphasize | ✓ | | ✓ | | | | | |
| To deemphasize | | ✓ | | | | | | |
| To add interest | ✓ | | | ✓ | | | | |
| To provoke thought | | | | ✓ | ✓ | | | |
| To clarify | ✓ | | ✓ | ✓ | ✓ | ✓ | | ✓ |
| To be polite | | | | | | | ✓ | |
| To show negative emotion | | ✓ | ✓ | | | | | ✓ |
| To guide another's actions | | | | | | | ✓ | |
| To manage the discourse | | | | | | | | ✓ |

learning to make literal statements is also important, avoiding figurative language will make your speech sound stilted. As a nonnative speaker of the language, you will first try to use figurative language the way it is used in your native culture. This can work to varying degrees, but by attempting to use figurative language early on, you will be building expertise in the social use of your target language, which will allow you to communicate more naturally, as well as to use this knowledge in a top-down way to learn even more about the language.

An example of a figure of speech that can be incorporated in foreign language learning almost immediately is the rhetorical question, which can be thought of as an insincere question. For example, a mother who asks "How many times must I tell you?" while scolding her child is not asking for an answer. In fact, answering the question will probably have the perlocutionary effect of making mom mad.

In many languages, the intonation for the words *yes* and *no* can be quickly changed to make a rhetorical question. This is true in English, yes? And of course, these types of rhetorical questions are very quickly taught and learned in most foreign language situations. Because using a rhetorical question adds an extra component to an otherwise straightforward literal statement, it accomplishes at least two conversational goals at once: making a statement and asking for agreement. In Korean, for example, one way of making a rhetorical question is as easy as adding "jyo" to the end of the root form of adjectives and verbs. This means that as English speakers learn Korean, when they learn how to say that something is pretty, or interesting, or complicated, they can also practice using these words in a more natural way than just making a literal statement ("It's hot" versus "It's hot, don't you think?")—thereby greatly increasing the number of situations that students of Korean can try out their newly learned vocabulary words on unsuspecting native speakers.

Let's look at another figure of speech: idiomatic expressions. An idiom can be thought of as a "frozen" metaphor. That is, over time, the more a metaphor is used, the less malleable it becomes. Of course, the first time someone learning English encounters an idiomatic expression such as *kick the bucket* to mean "die," it will seem novel.[9] But if a student learning English treats the idiom as if it's not frozen and mistakenly says *kick the can* to mean "die", he will not be understood. Note that part of learning the idiom *kick the bucket* includes learning when and where to use it. It might be more appropriate to use in reference to a despised dictator but not a beloved relative.

Although, as we noted earlier, rote memorization is not a strength of the adult language learner, idiomatic expressions are well worth the effort to acquire. Because idiomatic expressions can be used in a variety of settings, taking the time to learn these expressions can really pay off. For example, the linguistic equivalent of *we're all in the same boat* will be helpful in a large number of situations, making your linguistic output much more interesting than merely saying something like *same same*.

In addition, knowing idiomatic expressions will give you insight into the culture. For example, in Korean the equivalent of the expression *pie in the sky* can be translated as "a picture of a rice cake." This idiomatic expression is quite easy to memorize in Korean, since students of Korean learn the word for rice cake early in their studies. The word for picture is also a basic vocabulary word. It takes virtually no cognitive effort to join these two previously learned vocabulary words into the idiomatic expression, and can be done quite early in the language learning process. Waiting to learn this idiom until much later deprives the student of an easy way to increase proficiency and show cultural awareness.

One of the frustrations of the adult foreign language learner is that it takes a long time before he or she begins speaking and sounding like an adult. All too often, adult language learners lament the fact that they sound like a three-year-old—or worse yet, envy the three-year-old her fluency. Improving the "metaphoric intelligence" of a foreign language learner not only leads to better communicative effectiveness, it also serves to reinforce pronunciation, vocabulary, and grammatical structures in a natural and sophisticated way, and highlights cultural norms that are essential to language use.[10] It's also nice to speak like a grown-up.

**Don't Be a Language Zombie**

Although it is beyond the scope of this book to describe all of the ways in which language interacts with culture, the social use of language is more than just accomplishing goals; it also includes using the language to maintain interpersonal relationships.[11] If you ignore this fact, all the esoteric vocabulary and sophisticated grammar in the world can't save you from making some serious blunders.

For example, Americans are uncomfortable with silence in a way that people from many other cultures are not. And because Americans don't like silence, they talk in order to fill it. Americans talk to strangers in elevators. They talk to people in line at the grocery store. They talk to the clerk at the grocery store. They talk to their seatmates on airplanes. They even feel the need to get in the last word by saying "Have a nice day" at the end of the most mundane interactions.

Americans have words to describe this kind of talk: "meaningless conversation," "shooting the breeze," "idle chitchat," "or "passing the time." And all this empty chatter works just fine—as long as the other person is aware of what is going on.

But all too often, Americans fail to recognize that this empty, silence-filling banter is not always meaningless to non-Americans. At best, exchanging pleasantries with perfect strangers in another country will be seen as quaint or quintessentially American. Unfortunately, it may also lead them to think of Americans as rude, overly forward, or insincere; in many cultures, unlike the United States, any conversation—regardless of length or content—implies an attempt at establishing intimacy or closeness.

For example, two Americans can sit next to each other on a flight from New York to San Francisco and for the next five hours share secrets they wouldn't tell their therapists. But when they get off the plane in San Francisco, they may not know each other's names. And because they are Americans, *not* seeing each other again would feel perfectly natural, and possibly even desirable.

But if an American sits next to someone from another country, and chats pleasantly with him throughout the flight, it is possible that, by the time the plane lands, the non-American will want to figure out when they can meet again. This is because what seemed like idle conversation to the American was seen by the non-American as a sincere desire to establish a closer bond. And if the American doesn't try to maintain the relationship, she might be viewed as superficial or phony. But of course, at the beginning of the flight, if the non-American didn't respond to the American's overtures at idle chitchat, he might be viewed as rude, cold, or standoffish.

As this example shows, interpersonal abilities that are finely tuned to one culture do not necessarily translate fully to another.

Some adjustment is usually required. A convenient way to think about cultural differences that influence language use is to consider whether a culture is a *high-context culture* or a *low-context culture*.[12]

High-context cultures include Japan, China, and Korea. With regard to pragmatics, individuals from high-context cultures leave many things unsaid, since virtually all speakers of the language share the same cultural context.[13] Put another way, since there is so much overlapping common ground among the speakers in a high-context culture, it is redundant, ridiculous, or rude to point out the obvious. Speakers from high-context cultures speak sparingly, therefore, using silence to convey meaning. Such a speech style sets up an "in group" versus an "out group" linguistic environment. For example, in Japanese, Korean, and Chinese a common term for *foreigner* directly translates as "outside country person." Furthermore, Koreans so routinely refer to Korea as "our country," that when Americans similarly try to refer to the US as "our country," they are often misunderstood as also meaning Korea.

On the other hand, individuals from low-context cultures, such as Germany, Norway, and the US, cannot assume much overlap in the common ground of other speakers of the same language. Therefore, background information must be made explicit. Interestingly, one reason schizophrenic language is considered incoherent is because people with schizophrenia often fail to take into consideration the common ground that is shared between themselves and their conversational partners. Schizophrenic language generally becomes more intelligible as those with schizophrenia and their conversational partners spend more time together, which presumably happens because common ground is increasing.[14]

Of course, we are speaking here in broad generalities, since describing a culture as being high context or low context in no way describes all of the people in that culture. Nevertheless, adult language learners from a low-context, or relatively low-context, culture must make adjustments to their interpersonal style when they move to a higher-context culture. They must be prepared for the fact that much background information will be implicit, that their use of the language makes them an outsider, and that they may be considered rude if they ask too many questions or try to get to the bottom of an issue. Likewise, moving from one high-context culture to another high-context culture also requires adjustment, since important contextual cues that go unsaid will differ between the two high-context cultures. Perhaps only when one moves from one low-context culture to another low-context culture is there less of a requirement for any pragmatic adjustment. In this case, the two linguistic environments match in that both require substantial amounts of background information to be made explicit.

Of course, there are bound to be personal differences in adaptation to a new culture. One way to increase adjustment may be to seek out cultural contexts that match one's personality. Expatriates whose personal characteristics match the predominant personality type of a target culture show better adjustment than those whose personalities do not match. For example, on average, people in Turkey are more extroverted than people in Japan.[15] This suggests that an introvert might adjust better to living in Japan than in Turkey.

What does all this mean for learning a new language? It may seem odd, but as you speak your target language, you are creating a lens through which others will view you. In other words, others can't separate "you" from "you speaking your target language." Even the world-renowned author Mark Twain, when he went to Germany, found that he had created a separate identity for himself as a German speaker, and wrote about it to comic effect in his essay *The Awful German Language*.

Your goal, therefore, should be to create for yourself a linguistic competency that takes into account your own unique relationship to the target language and culture.[16] The goal is not to mimic native speakers, but to express yourself as best you can while maintaining an identity apart from the target culture. If you don't do this, then you may be viewed as attempting to pass yourself off as a native speaker, which others may find laughable at best and offensive at worst. The onus is on you, therefore, to make any needed cultural adjustments through your use of the language. In other words, foreign language learners should make pragmatic choices consistent with who they are in the cultural context rather than duplicate precisely the pragmatic choices of native speakers. It is entirely possible that mimicking native speakers' pragmatic use of the language will lead to alienation.

In a similar way, cognitive scientists who study artificial intelligence have noticed that people find it disquieting when a robot's appearance matches that of humans too closely. This phenomenon is known as the *uncanny valley*, because graphs that plot emotional responses to a robot's appearance show a marked dip in how comfortable people are with robots that are almost, but not completely, lifelike.[17] This drop in comfort level is similar to that of people's repulsion to corpses and zombies. The goal of pragmatic mastery, therefore, should be *not* to impersonate a native speaker. You don't want to be accused of being a language zombie.

As we hope these examples have shown, an adult language learner's superior metapragmatic skills are more important than correctly conjugating an irregular verb or remembering an obscure vocabulary word. Don't make the mistake of *not* capitalizing on the interpersonal skills you've honed over a lifetime in learning a new language and culture.

# 5   Language and Perception

## Speed versus Accuracy

How would Alex Trebek, the long-time host of the quiz show *Jeopardy!*, fare if he were a contestant on his own program? When asked this question, Trebek, who was born in 1940, has replied that in terms of general knowledge, he would know many of the correct responses, but that he would be too slow to ring in and answer before his younger opponents.

This observation by Trebek highlights an important way in which younger and older adults perform on various tasks. Children and adolescents tend to have superior motor responses, while adults may react more slowly, but they can bring to bear general world knowledge that younger people may lack.

Research by cognitive scientists on this topic largely agrees with the intuitions that most of us have about speed and accuracy in adulthood. Timothy Salthouse, for example, has proposed a general slowing hypothesis, which links a decrease in reaction time in older adults with a general decline in the speed of information processing in the cognitive system.[1] This decline manifests itself in a variety of ways, such as more "tip of the tongue" states in middle and older adulthood, which we will discuss in chapter 8.

The slowing that adults experience has a variety of important implications for the adult foreign language learner, particularly in the classroom and in interacting with native speakers. In foreign language classes, instructors frequently employ a *cued response* technique. That is, the teacher will point to a student, and then the student is expected to quickly provide an appropriate response. This can be an effective way of keeping the students' attention, and a rapid-paced, dynamic approach can certainly make a class feel more engaging. However, an adult who has returned to the classroom after several years away may find herself not keeping up with her younger counterparts by being able to respond as quickly as they can. She may know just as much as they do (or even more), but she may not be able to articulate a reply as swiftly.

In a similar way, conversations between native speakers are marked by very short pauses between turns. The average length of these pauses is only a few tenths of a second. It is amazing to consider how much cognitive processing takes place over such a short period of time: the conversational partner's statement has to be comprehended, a suitable response must be crafted, and the motor program to articulate the words has to be initiated. However, all of this is going to be slower for the nonnative, nonfluent speaker. As a result, a short pause may occur in the language student's speech, and this may be interpreted by the native conversational partner as hesitancy or even a lack of cooperativeness.[2]

So what is the relatively slower, nonnative speaker to do? The best advice is don't pressure yourself—expect that your replies will take longer, and allow yourself the time it takes to respond. Of course, your conversational partner may not be so accommodating, and one way to deal with this is to learn a number of stock phrases in your new language that will keep your partner from jumping in or (even worse) switching to your native language. Examples in English include "Let me see," or "Hold on," or "Just a moment." This can turn the awkward interval into what linguists call a "filled pause," which prevents the exchange from being hijacked by your conversational partner.[3] Once again, we see how adults, who understand the ground rules of conversation, can capitalize on this knowledge to minimize the impact of being somewhat slower comprehenders and speakers.

### Can Learning a Foreign Language Prevent Dementia?

You may have heard that learning another language is one method for preventing or at least postponing the onset of *dementia*. Dementia refers to the loss of cognitive abilities, and one of its most common forms is Alzheimer's disease (AD). At this time, the causes of AD are not well understood, and consequently, there are no proven steps that people can take to prevent it. Nonetheless, some researchers have suggested that learning a foreign language might help delay the onset of dementia.

To explore this possibility more deeply, let's look at some of the common misconceptions about dementia and the aging brain. First of all, dementia is *not* an inevitable part of the normal aging process. Most older adults do not develop AD or other forms of dementia. It is also important to remember that dementia is not the same thing as normal forgetfulness. At any age, we might experience difficulty finding the exact word we want or have trouble remembering the name of the person we just met. People with dementia have more serious problems, like feeling confused or getting lost in a familiar place. Think of it this way: if you forget where you parked your car at the mall, that's normal; if you forget how to drive a car, that may be a signal that something more serious is going on.

The idea that dementia can be prevented is based on the comparison of the brain to a muscle. When people talk about the brain, they sometimes say things like "It is important to exercise your brain" or "To stay mentally fit, you have to give your brain a workout." Although these are colorful analogies, in reality the brain is *not* a muscle. Unlike muscles, the brain is always active and works even during periods of rest and sleep. In addition, although some muscle cells have a lifespan of only a few days, brain cells last a lifetime. Not only that, but it has been shown that new brain cells are being created throughout one's lifespan.

So, if the brain is not a muscle, can it still be exercised? Once again, researchers don't know for sure. There are now many computer, online, and mobile device applications that claim to be able to "train your brain," and they typically tap into a variety of cognitive abilities. However, research suggests that although this type of training may improve one's abilities at the tasks themselves, they don't seem to improve other abilities.[4] In other words, practicing a letter-detection task will, over time, improve your letter-detection skills, but it will not necessarily enhance your other perceptual abilities. Basically, solving crossword puzzles will make you a better crossword puzzle solver.

The best evidence that foreign language learning confers cognitive benefits comes from research with those who are already *bilingual*.[5] A bilingual person is someone who is fluent in two languages. (People who know three languages could therefore be called *trilingual*, but the most commonly used term to describe a person with three or more languages is *multilingual*.) Bilingualism most commonly occurs when children are exposed to two languages, either in the home (mom speaks Dutch, dad speaks

Spanish) or more formally in early schooling. But bilingualism certainly occurs in adulthood as well.

Bilingualism and multilingualism are actually more common than you might think. In fact, it has been estimated that there are fewer monolingual speakers in the world than bilinguals and multilinguals.[6] Although in many countries most inhabitants share just one language (for example, Germany and Japan), other countries have several official languages. Switzerland, for example, has about the same population as New York City (about eight million people), and yet it has four official languages: German, French, Italian, and Romansh. Throughout large parts of Africa, Arabic, Swahili, French, and English are often known and used by individuals who speak a different, indigenous language in their home than they do in the marketplace. So bilingualism and multilingualism are pervasive worldwide. And with regard to cognitive abilities, the research on those who possess more than one language paints an encouraging picture.

For one thing, bilinguals outperform monolinguals on tests of selective attention and multitasking. Selective attention can be measured by what is called the "Stroop Test" in which individuals look at a list of color names written in different colors. The task is to name the colors that words are printed in, rather than say the word itself. (If you search for "Stroop Test" or "Stroop Effect" online, you can take this test yourself.) Because we read automatically, it can be difficult to ignore the word "blue," and report that it is printed in green. Bilinguals perform better on the Stroop Test, as well as other measures of selective attention.[7]

They also are better at multitasking, or doing two or more things at once. When you're chatting on your cell phone and avoiding fellow pedestrians on a crowded sidewalk, you're multitasking. One explanation of this superiority is that speakers of two languages are continually inhibiting one of their languages, and this process of inhibition confers general cognitive benefits to other activities. In fact, bilingual individuals outperform their monolingual counterparts on a variety of cognitive measures, such as performing concept-formation tasks, following complex instructions, and switching to new instructions. For the sake of completeness, it should be noted that the advantages of being bilingual are not universal across all cognitive domains. Bilingual individuals have been shown to have smaller vocabularies and to take longer in retrieving words from memory when compared to monolinguals. In the long run, however, the cognitive and linguistic advantages of being bilingual far outweigh these two issues.[8]

If the benefits of being bilingual spill over to other aspects of cognition, then we would expect to see a lower incidence of Alzheimer's disease in bilinguals than in monolinguals, or at least a later onset of AD for bilinguals. In fact, there is evidence to support this claim. Ellen Bialystok and her colleagues obtained the histories of 184 individuals who had made use of a memory clinic in Toronto. For those who showing signs of dementia, the monolinguals in the sample had an average age at time of onset of 71.4 years. The bilinguals, in contrast, received their diagnosis at 75.5 years, on average. In a study of this sort, a difference of four years is highly significant, and could not be explained by other systematic differences between the two groups. For example, the monolinguals reported, on average, a year and a half more schooling than their bilingual counterparts, so the effect was clearly not due to formal education.[9]

A separate study, conducted in India, found strikingly similar results: bilingual patients developed symptoms of dementia 4.5 years later than monolinguals, even after other potential factors, such as gender and occupation, were controlled for. In addition, researchers have reported other positive effects of bilingualism for cognitive abilities in later life, even when the person acquired the language in adulthood. Crucially, Bialystok suggested that the positive benefits of being bilingual only really accrued to those who used both languages all the time.[10]

But as encouraging as these kinds of studies are, they still have not established exactly how or why differences between bilinguals and monolinguals exist. Because these studies looked back at the histories of people who were already bilingual, the results can only say that a difference between the two groups was found, but not why that difference occurred. Further research is needed to determine what caused the differences in age of onset between the two groups.[11]

Other studies of successful aging suggest that being connected to one's community and having plenty of social interaction is also important in forestalling the onset of dementia. Once again, however, the results are far less clear than the popular media might lead you to believe. Older individuals who lead active social lives are, almost by definition, healthier than their counterparts who rarely leave their homes or interact with others. So we can't really say whether being socially active prevents the onset of dementia, or if people who don't have dementia are more likely to be socially active.[12]

But even if studying a foreign language is not a magical cure-all, there is one thing it will do: it will make you a better speaker of a foreign language. Doing that confers a whole host of advantages we do know about.

### Generalization Is for the Birds

One of the most important aspects of achieving foreign language fluency is being able to understand the spoken language of others. At first, this can be extremely challenging, because without knowing the individual words in the language, it's hard to break up the steady stream of sound into units of meaning. Think about the last time you heard a foreign language speaker being interviewed on TV or the radio. You probably had the subjective impression that the individual was speaking very rapidly—much faster than a speaker of your native language, for example. And while there is variation across the world's languages in how rapidly they're spoken (measured in words per minute), the differences are not all that large. For example, the spontaneous rate of speech is about the same in English as it is in Japanese.[13] However, most English speakers would claim that Japanese speakers talk much more rapidly than they themselves do (and vice versa). Why might this be?

It turns out that when listening to one's native language, a powerful perceptual illusion occurs: it sounds like the speaker is pausing slightly after every word she utters. But. Nobody. Really. Talks. Like. This. Do. They? Since native speakers know the words of their mother tongue, their perceptual and cognitive systems are able to *segment* the sounds into discrete words. And at first, no similar segmentation can occur in a foreign language, because the language learner lacks the relevant vocabulary. The steady rush of sound without any perceptual landmarks creates the illusion of very rapid speech. As time goes by, however, it's possible for the perceptual system to train itself to pluck individual words out of this acoustic stream. This capacity for perceptual generalization isn't unique to foreign language learning, either: it occurs in any domain in which we gradually acquire expertise.

Imagine that you've decided to take up bird watching. At first, you would find the process of identification to be extremely challenging—all small brown birds might look alike to you.

Assuming that you don't give up out of sheer frustration, you would gradually learn to look for certain distinctive characteristics, such as the size and shape of the bird's head, the length of its wings or legs, and the appearance of its bill. You might also use other factors as clues, like the bird's song or its behavior. Eventually, you would reach a point where you could successfully identify a bird based on its unique combination of characteristics.

The thing is, you can achieve this kind of acuity only by looking at a *lot* of different birds. To continue with this example, you really can't learn to identify birds by merely studying individual illustrations of species in a field guide. This might work for distinctive species, but what about what birders call a "little brown job," which might be a sparrow, warbler, wren, or finch? Birds are small and active, and the lighting for viewing them is often far from ideal. Birders discover that they need to see a lot of individual sparrows to be able to differentiate them from other, similar looking species. In other words, the more sparrows you see, the better you'll be able to truly *see* them.

This same process of perceptual generalization occurs in foreign language learning. You might think, for example, that one of the best ways to learn a new language is to listen to the same native speaker over an extended period of time. But that's like studying one illustration of a sparrow—out in the wild, the real sparrows may look quite different. You will certainly begin to develop a feel for the language's sounds and rhythms by repeatedly listening to one voice, but you may end up with relatively poor *transfer*, which in this case would be the comprehension of speakers you've never heard before. After all, your goal is to understand the diverse individuals you may encounter in your travels abroad, and not just one speaker whose recordings you have repeatedly listened to. That would be like a speaker of Spanish listening to the speeches of Winston Churchill and expecting to comprehend London cab drivers and Glasgow shopkeepers.

Researchers have demonstrated this phenomenon of generalization and transfer in a number of studies. Ann Bradlow and Tessa Bent, for example, asked native English participants to listen to multiple speakers of Chinese-accented English. Later, these participants were exposed to another speaker of Chinese-accented English whom they had not heard previously. The participants' ability to understand this new speaker was greater than it was for another group of participants who were only exposed to a single speaker of Chinese-accented English.[14]

This generalization effect even holds true for native dialects of the same language. Do you think you would perform better, for example, at the task of identifying someone as being from Boston if you'd only ever heard one other speaker from that city, or many other speakers? Cynthia Clopper and David Pisoni explored this issue by asking participants to classify multiple speakers according to the region of the United States the speakers were from. When exposed to new speakers, the participants were better able to classify the speakers' dialects than a second group of participants who had been exposed to only one speaker from a particular region.[15]

It should now be apparent that the traditional method of classroom language instruction is less than ideal for perceptual generalization. In many classes, foreign language students are rarely exposed to much diversity with regard to speakers of the target language. And this constancy doesn't provide the perceptual system with the variability that is necessary to comprehend a speaker of French, as opposed to how *your* instructor speaks French.

Fortunately, there are many activities you can engage in to foster perceptual generalization in your new language. Although you may have just one instructor, you can expose yourself to actors in films, characters in TV series, and YouTube videos. In fact, the Internet provides you with an unlimited number of native speakers to hone your generalization skills. Your goal should be to hear as many native speakers as you possibly can. Even if you're a relative novice to the language, don't despair— just let the language in a video or play or a recording wash over you. Although this can't be the only technique you rely on to learn a foreign language, the important point is to provide the perceptual system with the raw material necessary to work its generalization magic.

## Acquiring an Accent

Foreign language acquisition typically requires mastering phonemes that do not exist in your native tongue. A phoneme, as you may recall, is a meaningful difference in sound within a particular language. The phonemic inventory of English contains about forty sounds. Some languages get by with relatively few phonemes (Hawaiian is famous for having only thirteen), whereas some African languages have more than a hundred. Unfortunately, your ability to produce or to even hear these phonemic distinctions gets more difficult with age. Let's see why.

By convention, phonemes are designated by letters or other symbols between forward slashes. So the /p/ in "pin" and /b/ in "bin" are phonemic in English—changing the initial sounds in these words changes their meaning from a metal peg to a receptacle for storing things. Other sound differences in English are *not* phonemic. For example, there are two versions of /p/, and the way they are pronounced depends on the context. When /p/ is word initial, as in "pin," a little puff of air follows the production of /p/. This is called *aspiration*, and it *doesn't* occur when /p/ occurs in other positions, as in the word "spin." (You can prove this to yourself by saying "pin" and "spin" over and over into your raised palm—you'll feel the puff of air in the first case, but not in the second.) If you are a native speaker of English, as a young child you acquired this rule implicitly, although you were probably unaware of any such distinction until now. In a similar way, speaking with a hoarse voice or a stuffy nose changes the sounds of the words you utter, but not the meaning of what you say. You simply sound like a person with a cold.

Things become more complicated when you must master the phonemes in a foreign language. Some of these sounds will be more difficult to acquire than others. The French and Czech /r/ would be examples of sounds that English speakers find troublesome, and mastering Arabic requires producing sounds much farther back in the vocal tract than is typical for many of the world's languages.

Although some adult learners of a foreign language do master nonnative sounds, most speak with an accent. But even native speakers of a language do not all speak it the same way. English speakers from Melbourne, Memphis, and Manchester will sound quite different from each other.

Perhaps you're thinking, "If only I had started learning a foreign language when I was in college, or even if I had stuck with it in high school, then I wouldn't sound like a nonnative speaker." The truth of the matter is that even starting in high school still might have been too late. In a study conducted by James Flege and his colleagues, South Koreans who came to the United States as children were assessed with regard to their fluency in English phonology. The participants heard an English sentence, modeled for them by a native speaker, and then were asked to repeat it. These productions were recorded, and judged by native English speakers on a nine-point scale, ranging from "very strong foreign accent" (1) to "no accent" (9).[16]

The results of this study appear in figure 5.1. The native speakers, as one would expect, received the highest ratings—a few slightly below eight, but with the majority rated between eight and nine. Almost none of the native Korean speakers demonstrated that level of fluency. Even for those who arrived in the United States as infants, their foreign accent ratings were below those for the native group. And as the age of arrival increased, the accent ratings declined. Native Koreans arriving in the United States at age 10 received an average rating of 6 on the accent scale. At the age of 15, the average rating had fallen to 4. And those arriving at age 20 scored only a 3.

Although it may be tempting to conclude that these results are due to the fact that English and Korean are so different from each other, this is not the case. Later research on native Italians who immigrated to the United States revealed a similar pattern with regard to age of arrival and perceived accents.[17]

However, other aspects of language are less affected by age of arrival. Flege and his colleagues also assessed the Korean natives' mastery of English grammar. The participants were asked to listen to and make yes-no judgments about the acceptability of various sentences recorded by a native speaker of English. Half of these sentences were correct, but the other half contained grammatical violations. For example, some of the sentences contained errors with regard to past tense ("A policeman *give* Alan a ticket for speeding yesterday"), plurals ("Todd has many *coat* in his closet"), pronouns ("Susan is making some cookies for *we*"),

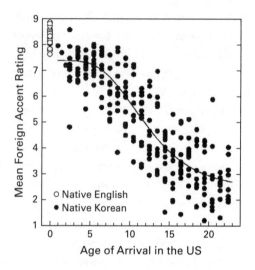

**Figure 5.1**

Reprinted from *Journal of Memory and Language* 41 (1), James Emil Flege, Grace H. Yeni-Komshian, and Serena Liu, "Age Constraints on Second-Language Acquisition," © 1999, with permission from Elsevier.

as well as other types of mistakes. Once again, a small number of native English speakers were also tested.

The results of the study appear in figure 5.2. The native English speakers, as you might expect, performed quite well: they all scored between 90 and 100 percent. However, notice that the Korean participants who arrived in the United States at the age of 15 scored, on average, only a bit below 80 percent. Those who had arrived at age 20 earned scores that approached 70 percent. However, when the researchers accounted for the number of years of education in the United States, grammatical ability was almost identical: 84 percent for those who arrived earlier in life, and 83 percent for those who arrived later.

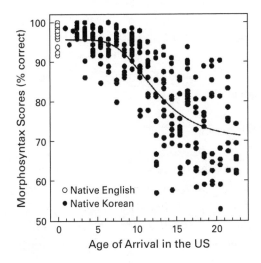

**Figure 5.2**
Reprinted from *Journal of Memory and Language* 41 (1), James Emil Flege, Grace H. Yeni-Komshian, and Serena Liu, "Age Constraints on Second-Language Acquisition," © 1999, with permission from Elsevier.

The underlying reason for these results has been the topic of considerable debate by researchers in cognitive science. Some have argued that the data are consistent with a *critical period* explanation, in which the innate mechanisms that allow first language acquisition in children decline steeply with age. However, if this were the entire story, then we would expect to see similar effects for the mastery of grammar as we do with phonology (compare figure 5.2 and figure 5.1). But that is not the case.

For adult foreign language learners, the results are clear enough. Although it may not be easy to achieve a native-like mastery of the sounds of a language, this does not affect the ability to approach native-like mastery of other aspects of the language, such as grammar. But if you speak your second language with an accent, this also means you've also acquired the language. Roger, who began studying German as a high school freshman, was once told by a native German speaker that he had a "distinguished, Hungarian" accent—which is far preferable to not speaking German at all.

## Can You Change Your Accent?

People seek out the services of speech-language pathologists (also known as speech therapists) for a variety of reasons, including problems with making speech sounds, stuttering, or stroke-related conditions such as aphasia. Because of their training, certified speech language pathologists are also qualified to help clients with accent reduction or accent modification. When they do, they help change how individuals produce sounds or how they stress words and phrases, or the rhythm of their speech.

Accent modification therapy is often sought by nonnative speakers who want to sound more native or by native speakers who want to get rid of a regional accent or dialect. In addition, actors preparing for a role may seek out this kind of help—although, rather than go to a speech language pathologist, many use the services of a dialogue coach to help them train for a role.

Because people who enroll in accent modification therapy are highly motivated to change the way they sound when they speak, it might seem that such changes would be easily embraced. But changing a person's accent requires an intensive amount of work, not only in how to physically make the sounds a different way, but also in how to cope with being a "new" person who speaks in this new way. The actress Meryl Streep, an undisputed virtuoso of accents and dialect, once said, "To capture how someone speaks is to capture them."[18]

In this book we make the claim that it is important for foreign language learners to start very early on establishing their own unique identity in the foreign language. After all, you are not just trying to communicate in a foreign language, you are trying to express *yourself* in that language—which is not the same thing at all. Even when students communicate adequately in a foreign language, they often become frustrated when they are unable to use the language to reflect their individuality, personality, or character. Learning new vocabulary words, grammatical structures, and pragmatic devices that are relevant to *you* will make it easier for you to speak in the new language and will help you establish an identity in that language. Getting rid of your accent will not help you do any of this, and in fact may have quite the opposite effect.

Accents, as one indicator of background and personal history, are a useful, necessary, and appropriate part of one's speech pattern. We argue, therefore, that not only is it a waste of time and energy to try to get rid of your accent, it is actually counterproductive. We recommend instead that you embrace your accent. Show it off! By considering your accent an asset, as opposed to a liability, you will have more incentive to speak the language—which will in turn improve your level of fluency and your confidence.

Clearly, if your speech is so heavily accented that you are unintelligible, or if your accent is so unusual that others focus not on what you say, but on how you say it, then you will need to work on improving your accent. Nothing is more frustrating than having to repeat a phrase or a word over and over—only to have the native speaker, when he finally does understand what you are trying to say, repeat it back to you in a way that sounds exactly the same. When this happens, of course you should pay attention to the subtle differences in pronunciation, stress, vowel length, or any other critical features that are important for your target language. But being able to articulate the sounds of the target language exactly like a native speaker is perhaps the most difficult part of learning a foreign language as an adult.

Rather than spend an inordinate amount of time fighting against your accent, it is much better to capitalize on your advanced metacognitive skills to analyze where and how it interferes with intelligibility. Then find ways to work around these problems, given the accent you already have. For example, you could learn another word that expresses the same idea, but which you can more easily pronounce. There is no reason why you can't choose words that fit comfortably into the way you speak. Or you can find a way to prime the listener for what you mean to say by providing more context. In Korean, for example, when Richard says the word for "translate" it often ends up sounding like the word for "violence"—and vice versa. But when he says "translator" it immediately becomes clear what he means because there is no such word as "violencer." Over time, Richard may get better at distinguishing between violence and translation—but until then, he can at least minimize the likelihood that he will be misunderstood.

There is, in fact, a word to describe foreign language learners who speak with an accent and choose for themselves the words, phrases, and pragmatic devices through which they express their own unique personality, even though this leaves their speech somewhat "foreign-sounding." They are called charming.

## In Praise of Nonnative Speakers

On May 29, 1953, Edmund Hillary reached the summit of Mount Everest. But he didn't do it alone: he was accompanied every step of the way by the Nepalese Sherpa mountaineer Tenzing Norgay. Why didn't Hillary climb Mount Everest alone? Because he needed someone who had previous experience climbing the mountain to help him navigate the dangerous terrain. In fact, at one point, Tenzing saved Hillary's life. Learning another language must also be a team effort, and ideally the person by your side has already climbed that mountain and can show you how it's done.

Unfortunately, one of the most common beliefs when it comes to learning a language is that it can only be learned from a native speaker. And it is true that learning from a native speaker allows you to hear proper pronunciation and phrasing in a naturalistic way. But learning from a native speaker alone is like being guided up Mt. Everest by someone who was born at the top of the mountain and is shouting directions down from above. The sounds may be pronounced correctly, but that won't help you find firm footing among the loose boulders and treacherous crevasses. What you need is a language Sherpa, if you will: a nonnative speaker who struggled with the language and who conquered it. This may seem counterintuitive, and it is not to suggest that learning from a native speaker is useless—far from it. However, there is much to be said for learning a language as an adult from someone who knows the terrain.

Richard studied French in many different places, but the best French teacher he ever had was someone who was born and grew up in the United States, a person who had fallen in love with France and the French and had learned the language as an adult. This teacher understood how Americans approach French. And therefore, he knew how to teach French to Americans. He understood fully why Americans make the mistakes they do, because he had made them as well. As a result, he was able to give his students insider strategies for avoiding these mistakes.

As metacognitive experts, adult language learners look for patterns and relationships among the sounds, words, phrases, and figures of speech in the target language. Therefore, it is important for adults to learn the target language from someone who can help them think strategically about it. Nonnative speakers who previously struggled with the language themselves often have insights into the language that native speakers do not have.

For example, when it comes to building vocabulary, although it's true that native speakers can tell you which words are common and which words are uncommon, they can't always tell you which words will give you the most "bang for your buck." Adult language learners, as strategic language learners, often seek out vocabulary words that can be used in the widest variety of settings. Experienced nonnative speakers will have discovered these words, and will already be capitalizing on them—and can easily teach them to you.

Strangely, in the US educational system, fluent nonnative speakers often teach children and native speakers teach adults. We feel that this trend should be reversed. Adults can do well if they learn from highly fluent nonnative speakers who also learned the language as adults. By contrast, children greatly benefit from being instructed by native speakers, since their ability to learn a language without an accent is superior to that of adults. The best advice for adult foreign language learners is to seek out fluent nonnative speakers of a language to help think about, and strategize on, the most useful words, phrases, grammar patterns, and figures of speech in the target language.

# 6 Cognition from Top to Bottom

## Hearing Is Also Seeing

In developing strategies to learn a foreign language effectively, it's important to be aware of research that shows that some of our intuitions about listening and speaking are simply incorrect. For example, when we listen to someone speak, the subjective impression is that our ears do all the work, and that our eyes play little or no role in the process of comprehension. Of course, even though those of us with hearing impairments can achieve impressive levels of understanding through lip reading, most people think of that as a special skill that has no relevance to how those with normal hearing make sense of speech. But in fact, we are *all* lip readers to some degree. Not convinced? Perhaps some examples can help.

A powerful demonstration of how hearing is also seeing can be demonstrated with something called the McGurk effect, named after (who else?) Harry McGurk, who published a paper on this phenomenon with John MacDonald (and like many important discoveries, it was stumbled upon by accident).[1] We're going to describe it to you, but we also urge you to look online for one of the many videos that demonstrate this effect. You can try it out first, or read about it and then view a demonstration. Incredibly, this is a perceptual effect where knowledge of what's going on doesn't alter your ability to experience a powerful illusion. Roger has shown this video to his perception class over several years, and is still amazed at how repeated demonstrations haven't altered his experience of the effect. There are several examples on the Web, but we'll describe the one that shows a long-haired, bearded man wearing rectangular granny glasses. You'll know it when you see it.

The video itself isn't much to look at. You'll see a closely cropped shot of the man's face as he repeats one syllable six times. There's a pause, and then the video loops back to the beginning. If you stare directly at the man's mouth, you'll hear him saying "da da, da da, da da." Watch the video closely for several moments to convince yourself that these are the sounds the speaker is producing. Now all you need to do is close your eyes and continue listening to the video. You should now hear something different—it sounds like the man has switched to saying "ba ba, ba ba, ba ba." But how is that possible? It's exactly the same video. In fact, if you open and close your eyes, you'll hear the sounds change depending on whether you're watching *and* listening, or just listening.

As you may have begun to suspect, there's a mismatch between the speaker's lip movements and his voice on the soundtrack. The man's voice really *is* saying "ba ba," but what you're seeing are the lip movements for "ga ga." This mismatch can't be detected when your eyes are closed, so you're able to hear the sounds accurately. But when you both hear and watch the video, the perceptual system detects a mismatch, and does its best to reconcile the difference between what is being seen and what is being heard. Your brain tells you that you're hearing "da da" because it's the best perceptual solution for the mismatched perceptual inputs.

By showing how vision and hearing can be tricked, the McGurk effect illustrates how the eyes and ears normally work together to create a more complete perceptual experience, even when we think we are just listening or just seeing. Because adult language learners benefit from having the fullest range of linguistic inputs possible, it is important to couple vision with listening during language learning whenever possible. Purely auditory learning materials by themselves provide a less rich, and therefore more challenging, learning environment.

For example, when we speak on the telephone, a great deal of the acoustic energy that differentiates one sound from another is simply thrown away, largely owing to bandwidth limitations. Early telephone engineers were relieved to discover that, even though the speech signal was altered, it was still intelligible. This is analogous to ripping a track from a compact disk with your computer to create a smaller MP3 file. It's possible to throw away the majority of the information encoded on the disk and still have a copy that sounds like your favorite song. That's because the disk's track contains extremely high and low frequencies that most people can't hear anyway.

What price do we pay for all of this compression? Not much, most of the time. Sure, your daughter's voice sounds a bit tinny and unnatural as it comes through the tiny speaker of a mobile phone, but you can still understand her without too much difficulty. But you may also recall other occasions when there *were* problems. If you've ever tried to spell something during a phone call, it's quite possible that the person at the other end wasn't able to completely understand what you were saying. The high-frequency information that the phone company threw away is the culprit. Sounds like /f/ and /s/ are rarely confused in face-to-face speech, because you can hear the high-frequency sounds that differentiate them. But, as we've explained, those sounds are being clipped severely in the transmission process, and the truly awful microphones and speakers in many cell phones don't help either.

So if you're sharing the news over the phone that your college-bound son was accepted by FSU (go Seminoles!), you may be met with confusion until you say something like "You know, *F* as in *Frank, S* as in *Sam*." There's a good reason why aviators and the military use phonetic alphabets (Alpha, Bravo, Charlie, Delta, and so on). Admittedly, most of us aren't trying to land a plane on the correct runway or giving orders over the din of battle, but the principle is the same.

You probably haven't thought too much about this because when you are speaking on the telephone in your native language and you experience difficulties, your prior knowledge of the language allows you to fill in any sounds that may be distorted or missing. Speaking on the telephone in your target language, however, means that you must rely more heavily on the sounds of the language only, since you may lack the contextual cues and background information that top-down processing would normally provide. Therefore, missing or distorted sounds or extraneous noise can easily derail your understanding in a language you don't know well.

You can experience another way that vision supplements hearing by watching television with the sound turned off. Tonight when you're viewing a favorite program, try watching it without any sound for a few minutes, say between sets of commercials. (If your family members object, tell them you're doing it for science.) Before you try it, estimate how well you think you'll do.

Most people respond to this question with very low estimates, and the claim is almost always the same: "I don't know how to read lips." If you're like many, however, you might be pleasantly surprised by how much you are able to understand. Granted, you will probably miss a great deal, but that's partly because of how most television programs are recorded. You're typically seeing individuals in profile as they talk to each other, so you're only seeing part of their faces. It's quite likely, however, that even with this impediment, you will be able to make out many simple one-word utterances, like "Why?" or "No!"

It's been said that you can claim to be a fluent speaker of a foreign language when you can understand a joke told in that tongue or understand someone over the phone. Understanding jokes requires cultural and pragmatic knowledge, but now you understand why telephone conversations, radio programs, and audiotapes can present such a challenge. Being aware of how hearing and seeing work together can help improve your language-learning strategies. For example, when you're having a conversation in your second language, look directly at your partner's face so that you can see her articulate the sounds that make up each word. Also, choose study materials that allow you to see people speaking directly in addition to hearing their voices. It's not always possible, and the effect may be subtle in some cases, but it will have a significant effect on improving your comprehension.

## Untranslatable

One of the great joys of learning another language is encountering new concepts. People take great delight in discovering a concept in one language that is seemingly untranslatable into another. This is especially true when it comes to emotion words. The artist Pei-Ying Lin mapped the relationship between some of these culturally specific emotions in an innovative project called Unspeakableness. One untranslatable concept represented in the Unspeakableness project is the Welsh word *hiraeth*, which Lin defined as "Homesickness tinged with grief or sadness over the lost or departed and the earnest desire for the Wales of the past."[2]

Based on words like *hiraeth*, linguists, philosophers, and others have wondered to what extent language influences thought. In other words, does the language one speaks determine how one thinks? There is no simple answer to this question. Fortunately, however, the majority of concepts needed to function successfully in a foreign language overlap with concepts used in the native language, to some degree. There is no reason to learn these concepts as if they were completely new categories. Adults already have very well-developed sets of concepts and categories that they express through their native language. Therefore, it makes sense to treat concepts from the native language as *prototypes* for the concepts of the new language, with the understanding that differences between the boundaries of the two sets of concepts will be refined over time through exposure.[3]

Put a different way, because words like *hiraeth* make up a minority of the many words one must learn in order to speak another language, whether growing up in Wales is the only way you can truly understand *hiraeth* is more of a theoretical, rather than a practical, consideration. To start learning Welsh, all you really need to know is that when someone talks about *hiraeth*, you know in general what it means to them.

This is not to say that the impact of language on thought is unimportant or has no real-world implications. For example, how individuals solve problems may be influenced by whether they are thinking in their native language or a foreign language. It appears that speaking in a nonnative language can provide a sense of distance from a problem that leads individuals to make moral decisions less emotionally. Other studies have also found that using one's native language to remember autobiographical events arouses more intense emotions than does remembering in a nonnative language. So be glad that there is not a perfect mapping between your native and target languages. The similarities are close enough to get you started, and once you're on your way, you'll enjoy the differences so much you'll never want to stop.[4]

## False Friends and Kissing Cousins

An overarching theme of this book is that the adult foreign language learner can capitalize on what he already knows to assist in the learning of a new language. When it comes to vocabulary, this turns out to be true as well. If the only language you speak is English, you might be surprised to learn that you already know dozens, and perhaps hundreds, of words in several other languages. This happy fact is the result of the unusual history of English. At its heart, it's a Germanic language, originally brought to the British Isles by invaders from what is now northern Germany and Denmark in the fifth century AD. Over time, this language, called Anglo-Saxon, became Old English, Middle English, and finally Modern English. Therefore, many of the basic terms in English are similar to words in modern German and the Scandinavian languages (which are also Germanic in origin). First-time students of German may be thrown by the idea of three genders for nouns or formidably multisyllabic words, but they will also encounter many old friends—*Mann*, *Vater*, *Sommer*, and *Garten* are all close enough to be recognized immediately as *man, father, summer*, and *garden*, to pick just a few of many possible examples.

This doesn't mean, however, that all similarities are helpful. Nestled among the words that seem so familiar to the native English speaker are a few that are actually quite different in meaning. They are often referred to as *false friends* (or more formally, *false cognates*). These exceptions can't be anticipated or predicted—they must simply be learned as exceptions to the general rule that similar-looking words are similar in meaning.

A German speaker who uses the term *bald*, for example, isn't referring to someone who's hairless, but is instead saying "soon." To the puzzlement of many a tourist, the *Menü* in a German restaurant isn't a list of all the dishes that the establishment prepares, but rather the day's special (*Speisekarte* is the equivalent term for "menu"). A *Puff* isn't a burst of air—it's a bordello. And perhaps the most famous German false friend is *Gift*, which certainly sounds like it refers to something pleasant to a speaker of English. In fact, it's the word for poison. Fortunately, the ratio of false friends to genuine similarities is quite low, but these exceptions are words to watch out for.

For many European languages other than those with German roots, it's still the case that your English vocabulary can be of considerable help. And once again, the reason has to do with the unusual history of English. What we now call England was ruled for half a millennium by the descendants of the Anglo-Saxon invaders, until they too were displaced by invaders from abroad. In 1066, William the Conqueror brought his army and his language to the British Isles. The invaders crossed the channel from Normandy, and Norman was a dialect of Old French. For several generations, the language of the ruling class was essentially a form of French, and what is now called Anglo-Norman was used for administrative purposes. The rest of the population continued to speak English (by this point, what we now call Middle English), but many Anglo-Norman terms found their way into the language of the commoners.

Traces of this essentially bilingual state of affairs can still be seen today in the unchanging terms used in legal documents. Expressions like *last will and testament, cease and desist*, and *aid and abet* are actually expressing the same idea in both languages. These so-called *legal doublets* are just one of the many ways in which the Norman invasion profoundly altered English. The advantage for today's speaker of English is the head start that it provides for learning vocabulary in many languages, and not just French.

To understand why this is so, a brief historical digression is necessary once again. Modern French has similarities with other tongues like Spanish, Portuguese, and Italian because they are all descended from Latin. Collectively, they're referred to as the *Romance* languages, not because they are necessary the languages of love, but because of their common origin in the language of the ancient Romans. Even Romanian, spoken in Eastern Europe and far from Rome, Paris, or Madrid, was once part of this empire, and is also a member of the Latinate family.

This means that many Romance terms entered English through Anglo-Norman, as new words replacing Germanic terms, or in many cases, taking up residence alongside them. As a result, modern English has many pairs of terms that are essentially synonymous—think of *moon* (Germanic) and *lunar* (Romance), and the legal doublets described earlier. These synonymous terms make the vocabulary of modern English unusually rich, and they also give the English-speaking student of modern Romance languages a considerable advantage.

And in fact, the news gets even better. Romance terms entered English through two other avenues as well. Latin was the liturgical language used in English churches until the separation with Roman Catholicism under the reign of Henry VIII in 1538. In addition, many technical, scientific, or medical terms were coined during the early modern era by drawing upon Latin (and, to some degree, Greek) roots. Latin was universally known by the educated class in England, so entrepreneurs, scientists, and physicians naturally turned to these word stocks to create new terms.

That's enough history for now—let's get back to the dividends that all of this will pay in learning vocabulary in other European languages. As an example, consider the word *hand*. We can readily identify it as Germanic, because this word is the same in modern German—*Hand*. And if you're trying to learn another Germanic language, the similarities carry through to those tongues as well: *hand* (Dutch and Swedish) and *hånd* (Danish and Norwegian). So you've always known this word in Swedish—you just didn't *know* that you knew it!

If we turn to the Romance languages, we can begin with the Latin word for hand, which is *manus*. This seems quite different, but it should remind you of English terms you already know— *manual* as in *manual labor*, or *manipulate*. And hand in the modern descendants of Latin is also recognizably descended from *manus*: *main* (French), *mano* (Spanish), *mano* (Italian), and *mão* (Portuguese). The terms aren't identical, but they have a family resemblance, and if you're on the lookout for such similarities, these *cognates*, as they're called, can be extremely helpful.

Even in cases in which a word doesn't derive directly from Latin, there can be a link if you know to look for it. In some cases, the common link is from the Greek, as in the word for heart, which is *kardia*. There are many English words and phrases that use this Greek root, such as *cardiovascular*, *cardiopulmonary*, and *cardiac arrest*. The Latin term is *cor*, which is fairly similar, and once again appears recognizably in French (*cœur*), Spanish (*corazón*), and Italian (*cuore*). More kissing cousins than brothers and sisters, perhaps, but the resemblance is still there.

Not only is this metalinguistic awareness helpful for many languages in Europe, but languages spoken in other parts of the world often have their own historical connections you can exploit. For example, many words in a variety of Asian languages, such as Korean, Japanese, and Thai, have roots in Chinese. Likewise, Russian, Polish, Bulgarian, and Czech, among others, are part of the same Slavic family. Connections among language families might not be helpful if you are studying one of these languages for the first time, but they will come in handy if you decide to move from Moscow to Prague. As mentioned earlier, there may be exceptions (so beware of false friends!), but an awareness of linguistic kinship will serve you well.

### Words, Words, Words

When most people think about learning a foreign language, they spend a great deal of time trying to tame the language's vocabulary. And although it's just one of many aspects of competency, it is undeniably essential—after all, one has to know the language's words in order to communicate. So let's take a look at perceptions and misperceptions of acquiring a new language's vocabulary.

One pervasive belief about foreign language learning is that you will have to master the pronunciation, meaning, and in some cases, the grammatical gender of thousands of words in order to achieve proficiency. This is such a daunting prospect that it probably scares away many would-be language learners. But it may not be as bad as you think. First of all, just how many words do you really need to learn?

If your native language is English, then you know that its vocabulary is immense: estimates range from a half million to a million words. Of course, this number is inflated by all sorts of factors: obsolete words, technical terms, and names for things rarely encountered (such as exotic plants and animals). All of these certainly fatten up the unabridged dictionaries of the language. It's also the case that, because of English's complex history, as described earlier, there is often more than one word that refers to the same thing. For example, both *kingly* and *regal* refer to the same concept, but you don't have to know both words to express the idea "fit for a monarch."

So if we factor out the obscure and the duplicated, we're left with a much smaller number of words than a half million. In fact, it's estimated that a native, college-educated speaker of English is unlikely to know more than a fraction of these—perhaps only about 17,000 words.[5]

How do you measure up against this number? You might think that the best way to determine to determine the size of your vocabulary would be to see how many words you know in a dictionary. However, this method would depend on the size of the dictionary. If you have a couple of dictionaries lying around your house, you can try the following experiment. Open the smaller dictionary at random, and point to one of the words defined on that page. Read it and see if it's a word you know. Now repeat this exercise nine more times. Multiply the percentage of words you recognized by the number of words defined by that dictionary (it's usually listed prominently on the cover). Now repeat the process with the larger dictionary. Do the two estimates of your vocabulary size converge? They're likely to differ substantially from each other. Although you probably recognized all the words you pointed to in the small paperback dictionary, you then multiplied the percentage by the relatively small number of words defined by that book. With the larger dictionary, recognizing even just a few of the words leads to a much higher score, since you're multiplying by a much larger number of defined words. So this method tells us more about the size of one's dictionary than the size of one's vocabulary. In reality, it's virtually impossible to accurately count the number of words in someone's vocabulary.

But if we can't measure the size of one's vocabulary that way, perhaps we can by answering a related question: What does it mean to "know" a word? The estimates of vocabulary size provided by researchers typically refer to a speaker's *receptive* vocabulary. These are the words that a speaker knows the meaning of, but might never actually speak or write. For example, when was the last time you used the word *microorganism*? You undoubtedly were exposed to this term repeatedly in high school biology, but unless this led you to a career in microbiology, you have rarely or never used the word since. So it's more accurate to say that a college-educated speaker of English has a receptive vocabulary of about 17,000 words, but uses far, far fewer than that on a daily basis.

And how about all of a word's variant forms? Should we count those? If you know the meaning of *help*, do you automatically get credit for knowing *helps, helped, helping, helper, helpful, helpless, helplessly, unhelpful,* and *unhelpfully*? Should this count as one word, or as ten (or more)? Linguists deal with this issue by designating one word as the *lemma*, or citation form (in this case, *help*). The other terms are considered to be variations of a single underlying *lexeme*. It is assumed that if you know the lemma, you also know (or can figure out) these variations.

And then there is the existence of what researchers call *frontier* words. These are words that you only partially know the meaning of. For example, you might know that *truculent* or *supercilious* are bad things to be called, but if someone asked you to provide their dictionary definitions, you might find yourself at a loss. Not surprisingly, therefore, the existence of frontier words greatly affects estimates of the size of one's vocabulary. If someone has a dim sense of the meaning of a word, does he know it or doesn't he? Clearly, the answer is not black and white.

Another reason why it's so hard to estimate the size of someone's vocabulary is that all of us speak in our own special way, which is called an *idiolect*. An idiolect is a native speaker's unique, idiosyncratic way of using the language. This is different from a person's *dialect*, which reflects the common linguistic features of a group of people. We all speak an idiolect and it includes not only vocabulary and grammar, but also particular turns of phrase. Idiolects are so specific that forensic linguists have compared a person's idiolect to a specific text in order to determine if the same person could, in fact, have produced it. This technique has been used to identify the Unabomber, the authors of the *Federalist Papers*, and the author of the book *Primary Colors*.[6]

If native speakers have a receptive vocabulary of about 17,000 lemmas in their idiolect, does this mean everyone studying a foreign language will need to acquire a similar number in order to speak a second language? Seventeen thousand sounds a lot better than a half million, but it's still a very large number. As it turns out, you can probably get by with less than a tenth of that. We know this because there have been several attempts to create a stripped-down version of English that can be learned more easily by speakers of other languages. In 1930, the linguist Charles Ogden proposed a vocabulary subset that he called Basic English. He suggested that a core vocabulary of around 1,200 words would be sufficient for communication for many purposes.[7] The fruits of such an approach can be seen in the Simple English Wikipedia, which (as of this writing) contains over 115,000 entries, many of which use only the words from Ogden's list. In the late 1950s, the Voice of America began to broadcast programs using Special English, which has a core vocabulary of around 1,500 words. So it is possible to communicate meaningfully with a relatively restricted number of words.

But is learning a language simply a matter of learning a certain number of words? We would argue, in fact, that the learning of words should not be seen as a primary goal in your attempt to acquire a second language. For one thing, most languages, including English, contain a large number of idiomatic expressions. For many such phrases, there is only an arbitrary relationship between the literal meaning of the words and what they refer to. We commonly use expressions like *kick the bucket* or *let the cat out of the bag* even though knowing what a bucket or a bag is has nothing to do with dying or revealing secrets. If your knowledge of a second language consisted only of what individual words mean, you would often miss the forest for the trees.

So while it's important to learn vocabulary, you will probably do just fine if you learn several hundred terms. If your primary goal is to communicate with others, it may be more helpful to concentrate on learning how to combine the terms you do know to make expressions that speakers of the language commonly employ. You'll be able to infer the meaning of many new words from context, and over time, you can develop an impressively large receptive vocabulary in your target language.

## Learning to Swim by Swimming

In an episode of the US television program *The Big Bang Theory*, the brilliant but eccentric physicist Sheldon Cooper is arguing with his long-suffering roommate, Leonard Hofstadter. To make a point, Leonard asks Sheldon to remember the time he tried to learn how to swim by using the Internet. Offended, Sheldon replies, "I *did* learn how to swim." Leonard points out that he had learned to swim on the floor. Sheldon replies by claiming that "The skills are transferable—I just have no interest in going in the water!"

This interaction is humorous because everyone knows how impractical and ineffective it would be to learn how to swim in this way. And yet many people learn a foreign language by doing something quite similar. If your goal is to converse with native speakers of your target language abroad, then learning vocabulary by listening to prerecorded lessons, flipping through flashcards, or practicing drills on the Internet is akin to swimming by moving your arms and legs on the floor. You might not drown, but you almost certainly will not give Michael Phelps any sleepless nights.

Just like for Sheldon, one of the biggest challenges for the second language learner is how to transfer artificially constructed language practice to the real world of language usage. In other words, how can we turn what we know into what we do?

Fortunately, cognitive scientists take an interest in the concept of knowledge transfer. Sometimes the transfer of what we have learned in one domain helps in acquiring new information. Noticing similarities in cognates is a kind of *positive transfer* if the two words in fact share a meaning. Sometimes, however, the transfer of learning can be *negative* if it interferes with acquiring new material, such as erroneously using the word order from your native language in your target language.[8] Clearly, then, the goal in language learning is to maximize positive transfer and minimize negative transfer.

There are two mechanisms that adult language learners can use in order to facilitate positive transfer. First, *low-road transfer* is reflexive and happens when well-rehearsed material from one context is applied to a new context. For example, if you've been driving a car for a long period of time, and now want to drive a rental truck, low-road transfer is all that is needed. This is the typical transfer strategy of many foreign language learners: repetition, repetition, repetition. Low-road transfer can happen automatically, but only with plenty of practice in a variety of settings. It is useful for scripted activities, such as greetings, politeness rituals, and goodbyes. Low-road transfer, therefore, emphasizes outcome over process.[9]

However, a potentially more powerful type of knowledge transfer is *high-road transfer*, which is mindful and relies on metacognitive ability to consider consciously how new material applies to both previously learned knowledge and future situations. High-road transfer requires actively looking for patterns and connections in the material, which will take time and effort. It's not as simple as merely rehearsing a phrase in a variety of settings. But the payoff is much greater because using high-road transfer will allow for flexibility in the use of the language. High-road transfer, therefore, emphasizes process over outcome. Consider the following example:

Richard and Roger once took a trip to Berlin, and as they prepared to leave their hotel room, there was a knock on the door. Roger, whose German at that time could be charitably described as rusty, opened the door and encountered a housekeeper, who asked him a rapid-fire question. He frantically tried to make sense of what had just been asked of him. Fortunately, Richard, whose command of the language was a little better, overheard the question and provided an appropriate response. As the housekeeper headed down the hallway, Roger finally understood the question. He was grateful for Richard's intervention, but felt quite foolish. He consoled himself with the knowledge that the housekeeper was probably used to dealing with tongue-tied foreigners.

How can Roger transfer what he learned in this situation to future interactions with housekeepers? If he tried to create low-road transfer, he could easily memorize what Richard said and repeat it over and over in many different situations so that the next time a housekeeper knocked on the door, he would be ready with the answer. The problem with this strategy is that Roger is likely to encounter some negative transfer along with any potential positive transfer, because it is unlikely that every housekeeper he encounters will ask him the same question.

Or Roger could recognize that low-road transfer won't help much in this case, chalk it up to experience, and not let it keep him from actively seeking opportunities to use his German on the rest of the trip, keeping in mind that learning German is a process, not an outcome.

But here's Roger again a few years later at a family reunion in Germany. This was a large gathering of distant relatives, and they were delighted that one of their American cousins was able to attend. The German typically taught in the United States is called High German (*Hochdeutsch*), which is the standard dialect. Therefore, Roger had studied only High German in high school and college. The family reunion, however, took place in a small city near the Dutch border. In that area, *Plattdeutsch*, or "Low"

German is the native dialect, although everyone is also familiar with the standard dialect.

At first, Roger was encouraged by his successful efforts to make small talk with family members at the breakfast table. In hindsight, however, these interactions were a sham: his hosts took pains to speak the standard dialect slowly and to use basic vocabulary. When these relatives were catching up with each other at the reunion, however, they were off to the races. They would occasionally interrupt their steady stream of excited chatter with guilty looks in Roger's direction, and would remind each other with the phrase *Immer Hoch!* to use the standard dialect. However, they would soon forget and lapse into Low German. Unfortunately, Roger didn't realize that when his relatives used the local dialect it was an excellent opportunity for him to take advantage of high-road transfer. He missed the chance to look for similarities between the German he had studied and the German he was hearing. As his relatives switched back and forth between German dialects, the differences he perceived in vowel pronunciation, word choice, and other linguistic features could have been applied to his future German studies. And, at a pragmatic level, Roger missed out on the opportunity to engage his family in a conversation about German dialects that he would have found both fascinating and instructive.

Of course, low-road and high-road transfer will both be useful in foreign language learning. However, since most foreign language students are already familiar with low-road transfer, actively creating opportunities for mindful, high-road transfer between one's native language and the target language will be time well spent. The main point about transfer, however, is not to be like Sheldon—afraid to get in the water. Dive in—even if you have to wear water wings.

## Metaphors and Idioms: A Free Ride or a Sticky Wicket?

Acquiring a second language presents us with many seemingly daunting challenges. We have to learn a different grammatical system. We have to master or at least approximate sounds that do not exist in our native tongue. We have to absorb the vocabulary of the foreign language, or at least several hundred words of it. Everything seems different. But in fact, one major aspect remains the same, and this is the conceptual structure that all languages share. We may need to learn that *dog* is *el perro* in Spanish, or *kutya* in Hungarian, or *inu* in Japanese, but the *concept* of "dog" remains unchanged. From a Mexican Chihuahua to a Hungarian Vizsla to a Japanese Akita, the collection of entities that this term includes (and does not include) is the same as in your native language. At its heart, a language is a shorthand for describing one's experiences, and since humans physically perceive the world in roughly the same way, most concepts are roughly equivalent. The ways in which this shorthand is expressed will vary widely, but a universal conceptual grounding abides.

You can leverage this conceptual core in many ways as you study a new language. It can, for example, help you make sense of metaphorical relationships. A *metaphor*, in case you're rusty with rhetorical terms, is simply a comparison between two things. *The road was a snake as it wound through the mountains* would be an example. The term *metaphor* is used when the comparison is implicit, as in the previous sentence, while *simile* refers to an explicit comparison, as in *The road was like a snake*.

A great deal of language, it turns out, is metaphorical. Sometimes this is obvious, as in the *snake* example, but often it is not. Cognitive scientists talk about metaphors as existing on a continuum of novelty, and at one end, many such expressions have become "frozen" in a given language. In English, we routinely refer to the *face* and *hands* of a clock, or the *arms* and *legs* of a chair, without even realizing that we are using the parts of the human body to describe the parts of other objects. And even more importantly for our purposes here, these metaphors tend not to exist in a vacuum.

The linguist George Lakoff and the philosopher Mark Johnson argued for the existence of entire metaphorical conceptual systems in their classic work *Metaphors We Live By*. They proposed that many linguistic expressions are based on particular conceptual metaphors, such as "Time is money" (*He spent the hour in the library profitably*), or "High status is up" (*She's climbing the ladder of success*). One of the richest examples of this argument is the conceptual metaphor "Love is a journey." There are dozens of familiar expressions that are unified by this conceptual core, and they run the gamut of emotions we experience in a close relationship. Consider the following:

> *Look how far we've come.*
> *We've gotten off track.*
> *We'll just have to go our separate ways.*
> *We can't turn back now.*
> *We're at a crossroads.*[10]

Seen in this light, it becomes clear that linguistic expressions may not be as arbitrary as they first appear. And this insight should provide you with some optimism about acquiring these seemingly disparate phrases in your new language.

Since we've been looking at metaphors concerning love, let's continue in this vein and consider some cross-linguistic examples. Many languages conceptually map emotions onto parts of the body, as in *to break someone's heart*. It would be discouraging indeed if this idea were expressed totally differently in different languages. Imagine if Germans referred to this as slapping some-one's forehead, while Russians made reference to punching someone's shoulder. Fortunately, across a variety of languages, the phrase is the same or recognizably similar. Germans speak of *jemandem das Herz brechen*, and the Russian expression maps equivalently as well. There are minor variations: Greeks would say that one "tears the heart," while speakers of Japanese would refer to this as "a thorn in the heart." In Spanish, there is still the act of breaking, but it's the soul instead of the heart.[11] Clearly, there is enough similarity here to be able to figure out such expressions when they are encountered.

Does this mean that we're home free? Unfortunately, there is another side to this issue of linguistic mappings, and it has to do with idiomatic expressions. Whereas metaphors wear their hearts on their sleeves (if you'll pardon the expression), the map-pings for idioms are often more opaque. A good example of this in English would be the euphemisms we use to talk about death. We might refer to someone as *pushing up daisies* or having *bought the farm*, but now the correspondence seems to be arbitrary. Nothing about daisies or farms seems to connect to death in a straightforward way, and so legions of students learning English have simply been instructed to learn such expressions by rote. They are what they are.

This notion, however, has been challenged by the cogni-tive scientist Ray Gibbs. He has pointed out that even relatively opaque idiomatic expressions may have a broader conceptual basis. Consider, for example, the ways in which we talk about someone becoming extremely angry:

*Blow your stack.*
*Flip your lid.*
*Hit the ceiling.*

*His pent-up anger welled up inside him.*

The common element in these idioms is a conceptual mapping of anger as heated fluid within a container.[12]

Obviously, not every such mapping works: it would sound odd, at least in English, to say that a deceased person is *pushing up petunias* or has *purchased the plantation*. This nonproductivity, as researchers refer to it, is why certain expressions are labeled as metaphoric, whereas others are idiomatic. A road can be like a snake, or like spaghetti, or like anything else that can be bent or twisted. Idioms are said to be frozen either because the conceptual mapping has been lost over time or never existed in the first place.

The important point is to recommend that you take a step back and think about the conceptual mappings of metaphors and idioms in your target language, which can help you to organize and remember those that you're learning.[13] There will be many cases in which these mappings won't work, but if you are alert to the possibilities of conceptual mappings, you can once again take advantage of what your native language has provided you for free. In addition, by learning the new conceptual mappings of your target culture, you will be able to use the language far more eloquently.

# 7   Making Memories …

## The Workings of Working Memory

Have you ever wondered about the length of telephone numbers? When the engineers working for the Bell Telephone Company created the modern phone system in the 1950s, they had to consider a variety of factors. If the numbers were too short, there wouldn't be enough of them to go around. If they were too long, people would make mistakes when they used them. (Remember that this was when calling someone meant repeatedly turning a dial with your index finger. It could take several seconds to dial a number, so mistakes were costly in terms of time wasted.) Most importantly, however, if the numbers were too long, people wouldn't be able to remember them. But how long is too long?

Let's try a little memory experiment. Before reading any further, hand this book to a family member or friend, and ask her to follow the instructions shown below:

*Please read the following numbers out loud. Speak the numbers at a rate of about four per second, and try to keep the pauses between each number the same length:*

3 7 2 9 5 8 1 6 0 2 7 4

*Immediately after you finish, ask that the numbers be repeated out loud. Now hand the book back (and thank you!).*

This is called a *digit span* task. Chances are, you weren't able to repeat the entire twelve-digit sequence. Most people are able to remember the first few numbers, but then, somewhere around the middle of the list, their memory collapses like a house of cards. Whatever the span of one's memory is, it seems to be fewer than twelve numbers.

Cognitive scientists have made use of this digit span test for a variety of purposes, but we'll just focus on estimates of its size for now. George Miller, who was in fact one of the very first cognitive scientists, famously referred to the number of items that can be held in memory as "the magical number seven, plus or minus two."[1] And in fact, the engineers at Bell Labs made use of Miller's research when they decided that seven digits offered the best balance between phone number length and people's memory limitations.

But just as some people claim that age is simply a number, it turns out that digit span is rather arbitrary as well. A moment ago, you probably failed in your attempt to recall a twelve-digit number that you'd just heard. Now we're going to give you another twelve-digit number, and ask you to recall it. And we confidently predict that you'll do much better with this one (here's a hint: think about dates from history):

1 4 9 2 1 7 7 6 2 0 0 1

How did you do? If you realized that this twelve-digit sequence is composed of the years of three important events in American history, then you could think about it as:

1492, 1776, and 2001

This sequence isn't just a meaningless string of digits. The first four digits are also the year of Columbus's discovery of the New World, the second four correspond to the year America declared independence from Britain, and the final four will always be connected with the year of the 9/11 terrorist attacks.

This would seem to contradict Miller's claim that the normal amount of information we can remember using the digit span task is seven, or nine at most. However, think about what you did for this second example: instead of passively listening to your friend, as in the first case, you imposed *meaning* on the numbers. And this makes all the difference. Miller called this *chunking*. So one's digit span isn't seven plus or minus two items; it's seven plus or minus two *chunks*. In his paper, Miller provided an elegant simile: short-term memory (as measured by digit span) is like a purse that can hold seven coins. However, the coins can be copper, or they can be gold.

If you think about chunking, then, phone numbers aren't really seven numbers long. This is because area codes are meaningful, not just random. For example, in the television show *Seinfeld*, Elaine was upset because she wanted to keep the traditional Manhattan area code of 202, rather than one of the newer numbers. For Elaine, and others, the area code 202 *means* Manhattan. So if an area code is thought of as one meaningful chunk, instead of three separate numbers, then even telephone numbers with area codes are still comfortably within a normal person's digit span ability of five to nine chunks.

Digit span is important for our purposes because it provides a way of measuring a person's short-term or *working* memory. And working memory is a key component of language comprehension. Spoken language isn't produced all at once: a speaker articulates words one by one over time, until his thought is complete. And when we read, our eyes jump from point to point on a line of text as we decode the words individually or in groups. In either case, it's essential to hang on to the first part of a sentence until the last words are encountered.

Working memory size is affected by many factors, such as intelligence (people with higher IQs perform better on digit span tests) and one's mood (clinically depressed individuals perform worse). However, another major factor is one's age. Memory span appears to increase during childhood and then plateau in the late teenage years. After the age of twenty, researchers have documented a steady decline, at least as measured by traditional digit span techniques.[2] So one factor that potentially makes language learning harder for adults is the gradual diminution of one's ability to hold several things in mind at once. This loss, while far from ideal, may not be as problematic as it first appears. Adults possess more general world knowledge than children, so they can employ chunking far more effectively. Age may adversely affect one's digit span, but knowledge and experience make it easy to compensate for this decline by making sense out of these numbers.

What does all this mean for language learning? Often in a language class, students are asked to listen to a dialogue or spoken text and then repeat back verbatim what they heard. This is a difficult task in the best of circumstances, and with age, the task becomes more difficult. In fact, even when people are asked to do this in their native language, they are often unable to do so. Native speakers will paraphrase what they hear—being true to the meaning of the phrase, even if they don't use the exact same words.

Therefore, when language learners try to memorize and then repeat long parts of a text verbatim, they are actually testing their working memory, rather than developing linguistic competence. Such oral drills and memorization exercises discriminate against the adult language learner. "The adult learns best not by rote, but by integrating new concepts and material into already existing cognitive structures."[3]

This is not to say that language students do not need to memorize anything. And it is also not to say that listening comprehension is unimportant. Of course, students will need to memorize vocabulary words and phrases. This is especially true for idiomatic expressions (for example, *letting the cat out of the bag* can't really be paraphrased as *releasing the feline from the sack*). But rote memorization of dialogue and text is a cognitively demanding task that will most likely frustrate the adult language learner. Rather than focusing on exercises that primarily tax working memory, we suggest that adult language learners acquire new vocabulary, grammatical structures, and idiomatic expressions by focusing on meaning. Learning to chunk seemingly disconnected words into meaningful units, and focusing on meaning through the use of paraphrasing, will make the time spent studying more effective.

As you may have guessed, the story of working memory is a bit more complicated than described so far. In fact, researchers are still debating the exact size of working memory.[4] But is a container metaphor the best way to conceptualize working memory in the first place?

The British psychologist Alan Baddeley and others began to suspect that working memory was more than just a temporary repository for things you've heard or seen. These researchers began a program of research in the 1970s that continues to the present day. Through a series of studies, they demonstrated that instead of being a monolithic structure, working memory actually consists of a number of cognitive subcomponents, the most important of which for our purposes is called the *central executive*.[5]

As we saw earlier, one way of thinking about working memory is to conceptualize it as a purse that can hold a limited number of coins. Baddeley, in contrast, conceptualized it as a workbench—a place where mental contents can be actively manipulated. Information from long-term memory can be called up from storage and brought into working memory to help with the task at hand (much like how you used your knowledge of American history to recognize significant years in our earlier example). Moving information to and from long-term memory is one of the roles of the central executive.

As you've gotten older, you may have noticed that you're more easily distracted by competing demands on your attention. For example, you may start one task, say, unloading the dishwasher, and then get distracted by a phone call or a televised news report playing in a different room. And after you've finished your phone call or watching the news story, you may have forgotten all about your original goal of putting away the plates and silverware in the kitchen. This kind of thing can happen at any age, of course, but research suggests that a culprit for those in middle age may be a decline in the central executive's ability to deal with competing information.[6] Just as a business executive might become harried as a horde of underlings make demands for attention and decisions, the central executive may find itself juggling too many tasks, and this can lead to making errors or forgetting.

Research suggests that the efficacy of the central executive reaches its peak during one's twenties, and declines thereafter, although perhaps not as much as previously thought.[7] This has important implications for the adult language learner. By its very nature, language production involves several cognitive processes unfolding at once. When you are speaking, for example, you must keep track of what you're trying to say, retrieving the appropriate words from memory and monitoring your listener's face for signs of comprehension or confusion. Although this process may seem almost effortless in one's native language, when speaking a nonnative language, the *cognitive load* (the amount of information that must be processed to complete the task) can severely tax the central executive.

Changes in the central executive also have implications for the process by which a new language is learned. Minimizing distractions and attention switching during study can decrease cognitive load. It's all too easy to check one's e-mail while completing a language exercise on the computer, but it would probably be best to avoid this kind of temptation. All of us seem to believe that we are efficient multitaskers, but the truth is that our ability to multitask is not as great as we think, and this ability does decline over time.[8] Finally, most foreign language materials are designed for high school and college students, and so they may be less appropriate for someone in their forties or fifties: the multimedia bells and whistles that are used to appeal to a younger audience may simply be distracting and unhelpful.

### Deep Thoughts

Our ability to remember our previous experiences can be quite impressive most of the time, but as we all know, it can also be rather fickle. Why is it, for example, that we can have trouble remembering something important, like where we parked the car, and yet be able to effortlessly remember the lyrics of songs that we haven't heard in years, and don't even like? Why do some things seem to "stick" in memory, while others do not?

An important part of the story may be how we think about the information that we later try to remember. According to an approach called *depth of processing*, one determinant of later memory is the mental operations that we perform as we learn something. In a classic experiment, Craik and Tulving asked participants questions about words that they were being shown. For example, participants might see the word cloud and be asked, "Is the word printed in capital letters?" or "Does the word rhyme with weight?" Such questions can be answered based on the superficial characteristics of the words themselves (how they're printed, how they sound), and without reflection on the words' underlying meaning. Therefore, only what is called *shallow* processing is required to answer the question.[9]

However, for other words, the participants in the study had no choice but to reflect on *deeper* aspects of the concepts that the words represented. To continue our example, some participants who saw the word cloud were asked "Is the word a type of fish?" while others were asked "Would the word fit the sentence 'He met a _____ in the street?'" It's impossible to answer these types of questions without reflecting, at least to some degree, on the conceptual characteristics of clouds ("they're up in the sky, not swimming in a lake or walking around on the ground").

After exposing their participants to a series of such words and questions, the researchers presented them with a set of words, and asked them to identify those that they had seen during the first phase of the study. Craik and Tulving predicted that participants' recall would be based on the type of task they had engaged in: Those who had been asked about *cloud* in the deeper conditions should have better memory for the word cloud than the participants who had been asked about *cloud* in the more shallow conditions.

As predicted, there was a robust depth of processing effect. For the participants who thought about whether the word had been printed in capital letters, memory was quite poor—these words were recognized, on average, just 16 percent of the time. At the other extreme, when participants were asked whether the word fit in a particular sentence, recognition accuracy was impressively high—90 percent of the words presented in that condition were recognized.

Although the depth of processing approach is not without its critics, cognitive scientists still draw upon it as a useful conceptual framework.[10] And it has important implications for the study of a new language. For example, many students believe that reading aloud in a foreign language improves their speaking and reading ability, as well as their expressive fluency. And while this may be helpful to some degree, it should be clear that this is a shallow task. Since the students are focusing almost exclusively on how to correctly pronounce the words, they aren't processing the texts deeply, and their memory for the vocabulary and the content of these passages will probably be quite poor.

In a similar way, the act of parroting back what has just been heard in a rote memory task is also shallow. It would be much better, as a deeper task, to paraphrase what you've heard, because in this way, you must grapple directly with the meaning of the words, and not just what they sound like.

Finally, some students believe that writing a word over and over creates "muscle memory," which may lead to superior retention for this word. Once again, however, such repetition is inherently shallow and fails to make contact with the deeper levels of processing that will create a more durable representation in long-term memory. Breaking the word apart into its meaningful components, for example, would be a deeper task. So a student studying German and encountering the word *Schadenfreude* would be well advised to try and recognize its component parts (*Schaden* = "to hurt," *Freude* = "joy") in order to learn and remember the concept's meaning (taking pleasure in the misfortune of others), rather than merely writing it repeatedly.

### Allow Me to Elaborate

The contrast between shallow and deep processing has implications for two different strategies that people use to try to remember information. Back when people had to call the operator for a telephone number, if they didn't have a pencil handy, they listened to the number and then just repeated it over and over: "555-1212, 555-1212, 555-1212" until the last digit was dialed. This worked just fine, unless the line was busy or the person didn't answer. In that case, they had to call the operator back to ask for the number again. (When Richard did this he would try to disguise his voice.)

Obviously, this strategy, which is known as *maintenance rehearsal*, is a very ineffective way to retain any information, and yet that is precisely how many people try to learn new information. They simply cycle it through working memory, never processing it more deeply. It's no wonder, therefore, that it fades so quickly.

In contrast, *elaborative rehearsal* strategies allow one to process information at a deeper level, more effectively transferring information from working memory into long-term memory. Elaborative rehearsal strategies include focusing on meaning. For example, to memorize vocabulary words, rather than simply maintaining them in working memory through repetition, better, more elaborative strategies would include paraphrasing, thinking about how the word connects to other words in your vocabulary, or thinking about how the word relates to yourself. Although you may end up studying fewer words per day, with elaborative rehearsal, the ones you do study will be more meaningful, and therefore more likely to be remembered and used correctly.

In addition, when rehearsing elaboratively, don't forget to take into account the zone of proximal development that was discussed in chapter 2. As you review information, such as vocabulary, grammatical structures, or idiomatic expressions, some items will seem ripe for you to learn. Pick this low-hanging fruit, if you will, and incorporate, through elaboration, the new material into what you already know. With this new, expanded knowledge, you'll have prepared yourself to tackle even more advanced material and expanded your zone of proximal development. In short, elaborate on what you know. As Ausubel famously advised: "The most important single factor influencing learning is what the learner already knows. Ascertain this and teach him accordingly."[11]

## Learning versus Relearning

Some of you may be reading this book because you want to relearn a foreign language that you studied previously. Perhaps twenty or thirty years ago, you studied a language in high school or college and would like to become fluent in that language now. But after such a long gap between the first time you tried to learn that language and now, could restarting on the language really be considered relearning? After all, it may seem like you've forgotten everything you ever knew about that language, and that trying to relearn it after thirty years would essentially mean starting from scratch. But is that really the case?

As it turns out, some of the very first studies ever conducted on human memory were about relearning. In the early 1880s, a German researcher named Herman Ebbinghaus examined the processes of learning and forgetting. This may sound a bit peculiar at first—you either know something or you don't, right? However, that isn't really the case. If you run into an old acquaintance on the street, you may be able to *recognize* him ("I know that face is familiar"), but you may not be able to *recall* how you know that person, or what his name is. In other words, memory includes both recognition and recall. In the case of recognition, all that's required is some feeling of familiarity ("I know that I used to know this person"). Recognition memory is typically excellent, even after several decades. Recall is harder, because it requires actually reproducing information, such as your acquaintance's name.

Ebbinghaus is famous for having proposed that there is also a third way of measuring memory.[12] There's recall and recognition, but there is also *relearning*. Ebbinghaus reasoned that if you are able to memorize something that you once used to know faster than you can memorize something that you've never learned before, then *something* must have been kept in your long-term memory—even if you cannot consciously recall it (like your acquaintance's name). We're going to describe one of Ebbinghaus's experiments in some detail, because it's historically important, ingenious in design, and directly relevant to our original question about relearning something like one's high school French.

To begin with, of course, Ebbinghaus needed to find something to learn. He didn't want to memorize meaningful material, like passages from books, because he was concerned that prior knowledge of the topic or associations to other material might make the study's results difficult to interpret. Instead, he invented and used an entirely new type of memory stimulus: the *nonsense syllable*. A nonsense syllable is simply a random combination of a consonant, a vowel, and another consonant, like *baf*, *zup*, or *tej*. These three-letter sequences aren't words in English (or German, for that matter), but they are wordlike in that they are pronounceable and can be memorized as if they were words. Importantly for Ebbinghaus, nonsense syllables have no prior associations, and therefore can be used as a measure of "pure" memory. Ebbinghaus created several hundred of these nonsense syllables, and inscribed them on cards to be used in his studies. (In a way, Ebbinghaus's method of memorizing nonsense syllables from cards is very much like foreign language learners' method of trying to memorize unfamiliar vocabulary words using index cards.)

Over a period of two years, Ebbinghaus conducted more than 160 trials of his experiment, using himself as a subject. Here is how a trial in Ebbinghaus's experiment unfolded. He selected one of his decks of cards at random (let's say it's deck no. 23), noted the time, and began to study the nonsense syllables. His goal was to learn them well enough to be able to recite the list from memory twice without making any mistakes. If he made a mistake, he would go back to studying the syllables until he was ready to attempt his recitation again. Eventually, he would achieve his goal, and he wrote down how long it took, which he called the *original learning time*.

Later, he would try to *relearn* the same list. He varied the amount of time that elapsed between the original learning and this relearning. The shortest interval was twenty minutes, and the longest was an entire month. In our example, let's imagine that a week has gone by, and he is trying to relearn deck 23. He did this in the exact same way as he had learned the deck the first time—and recorded the time it took. This was now a measure of his *relearning time* for the list.

As you probably have guessed by now, Ebbinghaus was an extremely dedicated and careful researcher. (He must have also been someone who didn't get bored very easily.) After two years of patient memorization and recitation, he had enough data to describe the relearning process.

Ebbinghaus quantified his performance by subtracting the relearning time from the original learning time, and then converting this number to a percentage, which he called his *savings*. When he looked at the data he had collected, he found that most forgetting takes place almost immediately (see figure 7.1). This forgetting curve shows that just twenty minutes after learning a list of nonsense syllables perfectly, his savings was only about 60 percent. After an hour, this number falls to about 44 percent. And after nine hours, the savings was down to 36 percent.

Now, if that trend were to continue, the result should be that Ebbinghaus would have forgotten everything he had learned in just a couple of days. But that isn't what happened. As you can see by looking at the chart, the amount that Ebbinghaus forgot, after dropping dramatically at first, began to level off. After one day, his savings was down to about 34 percent. After two days, it had dropped to about 28 percent. And after six days, the savings had fallen to 25 percent. After that, declines were negligible all the way to the longest time interval that Ebbinghaus used: at

31 days after learning a particular deck of nonsense syllables, he still had 21 percent savings (see figure 7.1).

Although other psychologists went on to replicate Ebbinghaus's research in different settings and with different types of materials, they all found a similar result—that although most forgetting takes place soon after learning, the material that does remain is available, even over long periods of time. Larry Squire and Pamela Slater, for example, studied participants' ability to recognize the names of TV programs and racehorses that they had been exposed to during a fifteen-year period (from the late 1950s to the early 1970s).[13] As Ebbinghaus would have predicted, these subjects displayed a gradual rate of forgetting over the years after having learned the information.

What should we make of this result? Like much of the research we discuss in this book, there is both good news and bad news. The bad news is that the process of forgetting kicks in immediately after we're exposed to something, and like sand

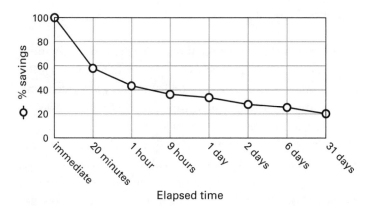

**Figure 7.1**
Ebbinghaus's forgetting curve.

through our fingers, most of this information just slips away. The good news is that this rate of forgetting slows considerably as time goes by. And keep in mind that this is just one way of measuring forgetting. As we will see, recognition memory can be excellent even many decades after learning something.[14] In addition, Ebbinghaus used nonsense syllables in his research. And although vocabulary words in a foreign language may seem like nonsense syllables at first, they eventually become associated with concepts and therefore stop being just "nonsense," which also makes them easier to relearn.

The encouraging conclusion for the adult language learner is that *any* previous exposure to a foreign language can be helpful when relearning that language. Although you may think that you have no memory for any of the vocabulary of a foreign language you learned in high school or college, that experience means that you'll be able to relearn those vocabulary words faster than someone who has never been exposed to that language.

### Cognitive Overload

Earlier in this chapter we mentioned the concept of cognitive load. As you may recall, cognitive load refers to how much information can be manipulated in working memory at a given time. We also discussed the ways in which researchers have tried to quantify exactly how much information can be effectively processed in working memory. Although estimates vary, one can easily see that the complex task of learning a new language places huge cognitive demands on working memory. When the cognitive load imposed on working memory becomes too great, we end up in a state of *cognitive overload*, which means that a person is no longer able to use working memory effectively to accomplish the task at hand. Moreover, to compensate for cognitive overload, a person may focus on simple aspects that are related to the task, but which do not actually add to learning in any meaningful way. For example, if you are listening to a person speak very rapidly in your target language, you may stop focusing on trying to understand what the person is saying, and instead focus on how they are saying it—such as paying attention to their accent or gestures. Clearly, cognitive overload interferes with learning.

Unfortunately, everyone learning a new language will experience cognitive overload. When this happens, it's important to recognize the situation for what it is and not to give up or blame yourself, the language, or the teacher. There are ways to manage the cognitive load that comes with learning a new language.

### Cognitive Overload from Factors Internal to Language

Cognitive overload can happen because language is inherently complex. Although not much can be done to alter the internal workings of a particular language, it is still possible to manage the demands placed on working memory that come from learning a language.

One way to manage the cognitive load in language learning tasks is to break the task down into smaller subunits that are easier to process mentally. For example, reading Japanese is notoriously difficult. But the task of reading Japanese can be subdivided. Because Japanese has borrowed more than 20,000 words from English—loanwords such as *conbini* for convenience store and *beddo* for bed—teachers of Japanese often start by having students learn these words. In Japanese, borrowed words are written in a special script called *katakana*. Katakana is the easiest of the three Japanese scripts for English speakers to learn because once they can sound out the word, they often (but not always) know what it means. In terms of cognitive load, learning katakana is less taxing on working memory than learning *hiragana* (which is used for purely Japanese words), or *kanji*, which are symbols based on Chinese characters.

But even with kanji, teachers can reduce the cognitive load of this task by showing students how to break apart the character into its component parts, which have somewhat consistent meanings across the characters in which they are found. This is the technique advocated by James Heisig in his book *Remembering the Kanji*. For example, the kanji for fortune telling is made up of two elements: "mouth" and "divining rod."[15] This is an example of managing the cognitive load that is specific to the language itself. To use Miller's terminology, the kanji for fortune telling has been transformed from five individual brush strokes into only two chunks, thereby increasing the capacity of short-term, or working, memory.

### Cognitive Overload from Factors External to Language

Cognitive overload also occurs when the way the material is presented imposes too great a demand on working memory. With any instructional technique, therefore, it is crucial to consider how each aspect of the technique itself requires something of working memory, and then reduce or eliminate those parts of the task that impose too high a cognitive demand. External factors that increase cognitive load include time constraints, motivation, distractions, and other situational factors that are not part of the language itself.

How much or how little cognitive load can be imposed before cognitive overload results follows a pattern referred to as the *Yerkes–Dodson law*. The Yerkes–Dodson law describes how, for easily accomplished tasks, adding cognitive load (or what we could also call arousal or pressure) is actually helpful in accomplishing a task. In other words, performance on easy tasks actually improves when external factors are imposed.[16]

For example, imagine that you are driving on Interstate 80 in Nebraska on a beautiful spring day. The road is dry, smooth, and there is very little traffic. What do you do? If you are like many people, you are likely to add cognitive load to this relatively easy task by singing along with the radio, or talking to your companion, or listening to a book on tape. In fact, because the task is so easy, if you didn't add any external complexity to it, your mind would start to wander and you could possibly fall asleep at the wheel. Therefore, adding extrinsic cognitive load is crucial to helping you accomplish the task of driving effectively.

But imagine now that traffic has suddenly gotten heavier, the sky has darkened, and rain is coming down so heavily you can hardly see the road. What do you do? The first thing you might do is to turn off the radio or tell your companion to be quiet—even though neither of those actions will make the rain stop or cause the traffic to clear up. But you do it anyway because the task of driving the car has just gotten more difficult, so you need to get rid of any unnecessary demands on your attention. If the radio kept blaring and your friend kept talking you might go into a state of cognitive overload with potentially disastrous results.

Here's another example. In the theater it is a generally held superstition that if a dress rehearsal is great, then the actual performance will be awful. But if a dress rehearsal is awful, then the performance will be great. Why? According to the Yerkes–Dodson law, if the actors and stagehands are very well prepared, then the dress rehearsal isn't stimulating and without the added arousal of an audience, they don't really try hard. The next night when the audience is in attendance, the added external arousal is exciting and they perform quite well. In other words, if you know something well you do better in front of a group than you do practicing alone.

Alternatively, if the dress rehearsal goes well without an audience, then the presence of an audience might add too much pressure, and cognitive overload may be the result. Therefore, if you don't know something well, you perform it better alone than you do in front of a group.

The same is true for language learning. As an adult language learner, it is important for you to control how much cognitive load you can tolerate before reaching a state of cognitive overload. If a task is easy for you, then applying it in ways that that add complexity will help you perform better. If the task is difficult, then it is important that you find ways to reduce or eliminate anything that adds unnecessary cognitive demands to the task.

Factors that increase cognitive load are often built into language-learning tasks on purpose to ensure mastery of the material. For example, teachers may give timed tests because the added pressure of a time limit will show how much of the students' language ability has become automatic. Timed tests can actually enhance the performance of speakers with a high level of proficiency, but they can impair the performance for those whose linguistic abilities are still shaky. Therefore, the addition of cognitive load cannot be said to be either good or bad. How a person responds to the additional cognitive demands placed on a task depends on the task itself, the cognitive strategy used to perform the task, and the individual's level of mastery.[17]

Interpersonal factors also place burdens on available cognitive resources. Even something as routine as being polite requires extra mental processing that can unintentionally cause confusion or misunderstanding.[18] In a similar way, if you are an outgoing person who is always looking for opportunities to meet new people, then a scavenger hunt in which you approach strangers in a shopping center and engage them in conversation will seem easy and fun, and therefore, you will not feel cognitively overloaded when you add to the complexity of the task by trying to engage them in your target language. However, if this is exactly the kind of activity you despise, then the added stress (e.g., overcoming one's natural shyness, or feeling embarrassed) could send you into a state of cognitive overload. In this case, the unnecessary external element (a scavenger hunt where you are forced to interact with unsuspecting strangers) artificially imposes such a huge emotional load on the linguistic task (which is, in fact, the main task) that it overloads the person's working memory capacity and very little learning will actually take place.

When designing or evaluating language learning tasks, it is important to think about the cognitive load required for the task. Try to separate the cognitive demands into those that are intrinsic to the language itself from those that are being imposed externally. No specific language learning task is right or wrong in terms of cognitive load—but some will impose higher external cognitive demands on working memory than others, which may, depending on the person, enhance the learning experience or create a state of cognitive overload.

### The Time-Traveling Intruder

If you've had to change your telephone number in the recent past, you may have experienced difficulties in remembering it at first. As you attempted to recall the sequence to answer a friend's query, your old phone number may have popped unbidden into your mind, and it may have taken some effort to recall your new number. This annoying phenomenon is a well-understood principle of memory called *proactive interference*. The idea is that old learning can get in the way of, and interfere with, your ability to recall things you've learned more recently. The more similar the old and new learning, the more likely it is that you will experience interference.[19]

Numerous laboratory studies have demonstrated the power of proactive interference—and most such studies are conducted on college-age students, so even younger adults have trouble with this. In a typical experiment, participants are asked to memorize a list of similar items. This list (we'll call it list A) might consist of words like *lion*, *giraffe*, and *elephant*. After learning list A, participants are asked to memorize a second list (list B), which contains items like *zebra*, *antelope*, and *gazelle*. After learning list B, participants are given another unrelated task, and after a few moments are asked to recall list B. As you might imagine, this can be a challenging task, because of the similarities of the words on both lists (animals that inhabit the savannas of Africa). Just like the old telephone number, the animals from list A intrude into the participants' awareness, making it more difficult for them to recall the animals from list B. Now imagine what might happen if participants are asked to learn list C, which *also* contains the names of African animals. The results aren't pretty!

Interestingly, interference effects can occur in reverse as well. If someone asks you for your current phone number, you can probably supply it readily enough. But if they were also to ask you to recall your previous phone number, you might experience some difficulty. In this case, the new learning—your current phone number—is causing problems for the old learning—the previous number. This is referred to as *retroactive interference*. Like a character in a bad science fiction movie, the new learning can travel back in time and make life difficult for information that you've learned previously.

As a foreign language learner, it's important to understand what causes interference effects, and what to do when you experience them. If you've been studying a list of Spanish nouns and find yourself making many mistakes as you attempt to recall them, you're likely to feel frustration. Instead of giving up, however, you would be well advised to shift your study to a different set of words, like adjectives or verbs, or to a different task entirely, such as grammar. When you return to the list of nouns, you may find that your recall has improved. Researchers call this improved performance in memory after a change in study material *release from proactive interference*. This suggests that it is wise to study different materials over shorter periods of time rather than one type of material over a longer period. For example, rather than study vocabulary for thirty minutes and then grammar for thirty minutes, it may better to alternate them every fifteen minutes and then take a break.

It may seem perverse that the knowledge you've taken pains to acquire in the past can sabotage your efforts to learn new material in the present or the future. However, that's viewing the glass as half empty. The fact that you experience interference means that you already possess a great deal of information in long-term memory. You're not just an adult language learner—you're a *knowledgeable* adult language learner. The trick is to make this prior learning work *for* you, not against you. First of all, be thankful that you have this prior knowledge and be glad that all of it hasn't been forgotten. Over time, information stored in long-term memory does fade, but no matter how much you may feel you have forgotten, as we mentioned earlier in this chapter, relearning is always faster than learning. If you studied Spanish in high school and twenty years later you decide to start studying Spanish again, you clearly have an advantage over the person who has never studied it, even if you don't think you do.

But let's say that you'd like to study a different language now. At first, you might experience some mild proactive interference. For example, the previously learned Spanish might interfere with the new language. As you continue to study the new language, acquiring more and more linguistic information, cultural knowledge and contextual cues, previously learned information will interfere less and less. Since you cannot actively forget information the same way you actively learn it, interference is normal and should be expected. Therefore, rather than berate yourself for the interference, leverage your metacognitive skills to exploit your previous knowledge and experience in service of learning the new language. For example, if you previously studied Spanish, but now you are studying Italian, apply what you know about Romance languages in general to Italian when and where appropriate. If you are now studying Chinese, there will be fewer ways to search out and benefit from such linguistic commonalities; however, because the languages themselves are so different, there is likely to be less interference anyway.

Because we are constantly learning new information throughout our lives, it is not surprising that older adults experience more interference on memory tasks than younger adults. The fact that it happens more frequently as we age merely means we've learned a lot more information. But even here, there is good news. Lisa Emery, Sandra Hale, and Joel Myerson found the expected increase in interference for older adults, but they also demonstrated that both younger and older adults showed complete release from proactive interference.[20] So when you begin to make more errors when studying vocabulary or grammar, just keep calm and carry on—but with a different task.

## Wait, Wait, Don't Tell Me

One well-studied memory phenomenon is the *tip-of-the-tongue* (TOT) state. This refers to situations in which you know you know something, and can almost retrieve it, but for some reason, you can't quite produce it. The researchers Roger Brown and David McNeill likened a TOT state to "mild torment, something like the brink of a sneeze."[1] You've undoubtedly had to endure conversations with friends in which they verbally flail in their attempts to produce something like the name of an actor. "You know, he was the guy who was in those *Superman* movies back in the Seventies ... and then he was thrown from a horse, and was paralyzed, and then later he created a research foundation ... you know, he was really tall and good looking ... what *was* his name??" (Just in case we've caused a TOT state for you, this example refers to Christopher Reeve.)

TOT states have received considerable attention from cognitive scientists because of their paradoxical nature: how is it possible to recall so much information about someone, but not the name? Fortunately, it's fairly easy to cause research participants to experience TOT states in the lab. Brown and McNeill discovered that if they gave their subjects dictionary definitions of rare or unusual words, they could frequently trigger the TOT state.

Before describing Brown and McNeill's results, let's see if we can put you in such a state. Below are a series of definitions based on their original items. After reading each one, assess what you're experiencing. There are three possibilities:

(a) You have no idea what's being described, and no feeling of familiarity. Remember that these are rare and unusual terms, so this may happen rather frequently. Just move on to the next item.

(b) You know that you know the object or concept being described, and can state its name out loud. In this case, you can congratulate yourself on your formidable vocabulary, and move on to the next item.

(c) You think that you might know the word, but you can't articulate it. If you find yourself in this state, we'd like you to guess (1) whether the word you can't remember is long or short; (2) how many syllables it has; and (3) what the first letter of the word might be. Even if you're not at all certain, just guess.

Ready? Here's the first definition (you'll find the answers at the end of this section). If you're in a TOT state, be sure to write down your guesses about length, number of syllables, and first letter.

1.   What is the name of the small boat seen in the rivers and harbors of Asia, propelled by oars and typically with a roof covered in woven mats?

2.   What is the name for the semicircular, vaulted area at one end of a church?

3.    What is term for showing favor in business or politics for members of one's own family?

4.    What is the name of the staff encircled by two snakes used as the symbol of the medical profession?

5.    What is the term for getting money or favors through intimidation or the threat of violence?

6.    What is the term for assembling people for a common purpose, such as a meeting or a conference?

7.    What is another name for a stamp collector?

8.    What is the term for displaying excessive flattery or an ingratiating demeanor?

9.    What is the name of the navigational instrument used for measuring angular distances, especially the sun, moon, and stars at sea?

10.  What is the name of the cavity at the end of a bird's digestive track?

We're hoping that you experienced a TOT state after reading one or more of these definitions. If you did, were you able to come up with information about the word itself?

Brown and McNeill provided Harvard undergraduates with such definitions, and found that they reported TOT states about 13 percent of the time. When the results were analyzed, Brown and McNeill found that the participants performed well above chance with regard to the three questions. Short words were believed to be short, the estimated length in syllables was frequently correctly recalled, and on many occasions, the first letter of the word was produced.

Even the errors from this study are of interest. For example, some participants produced the word *sexton* for the next to last definition above. "Sexton" (grave digger) is far removed from the concept of a navigational instrument, but identical to *sextant* in terms of length and number of syllables. They also share the same sounds. These observations provided researchers with valuable clues about the organization of long-term memory: it seems that words that sound alike may be stored near each other in long-term memory, and that certain attributes of concepts may be available even when others are not.

The adult foreign language learner can take away a number of important messages from this research. First, it should be comforting to realize that even Harvard undergraduates experience tip-of-the-tongue states, so you shouldn't get frustrated when this happens to you. In fact, so-called diary studies, in which participants are asked to record their TOT experiences, have found that these states increase from about once a week for younger adults to about once a day for older adults.[2]

Once again, these discoveries can be viewed negatively or positively, depending on one's perspective. It certainly is the case that such episodes become more frequent across the lifespan, but their presence should not be taken as evidence of a wholesale decline in memory. Although having a lot of knowledge does not seem to cause more TOT states, it should be reassuring, nevertheless, to know that when TOT states do occur, it's because the sought-after word is in fact present in memory, even if it can't be retrieved right away.[3] Such experiences often occur right before the word enters into conscious awareness, so if you believe that the term is on the "tip of your tongue," it really might be—you just need to be patient enough to allow it to make its appearance.

Answers to the tip-of-the-tongue questions:

1.  *Sampan* (some people think of *junk* for this definition as well).

2.  *Apse.*

3.  *Nepotism.*

4.  *Caduceus.*

5.  *Extortion.*

6.  *Convene.*

7.  *Philatelist.*

8.  *Fawning.*

9.  *Sextant.*

10. *Cloaca.*


**Practice Makes Perfect?**

A major part of foreign language mastery is practicing reading, writing, speaking, and listening in the new language. For many, the prospect of intensive practice will evoke memories of rote drills in a high school Spanish or French course. Most students find such exercises to be pure drudgery, and they can drain away all of one's interest in the subject.

Practice, however, really is an essential part of this enterprise, even if it seems daunting. It may be helpful to reflect on your goals for learning a foreign language. Remember, to do many things in a foreign language you do not need native-like fluency. For example, if your primary motivation for learning Swedish is to exchange pleasantries with you wife's extended family, then spending months in intensive study would be overkill. But to even do this, practice is an important part of the story. Our goal in this section is to review the cognitive science research on practice and expertise, and to offer some concrete suggestions about how to make the time spent on practice as efficient and productive as possible. You will learn how to work smarter, not harder.

What does it mean to be an expert? You may be surprised to learn that the study of expertise is an entire subfield within cognitive science. Researchers have studied individuals from diverse fields of accomplishment in order to understand how expertise is acquired. In the course of writing this book, we've spoken to many people who have asserted that they simply aren't good at foreign language learning; however, they based this perception on negative experiences in high school or college. This kind of reasoning illustrates a commonly held belief—that doing something badly once means to be bad at it forever, creating the conditions for a negative self-fulfilling prophecy.

One domain of extensive study has been chess playing. It's easy to identify chess experts, because good players will have a numeric ranking that objectively measures how good they are. There are a variety of such systems (the Elo and USCF systems are two of these), but the basics are the same. If you have a higher rating than I do, and I play and beat you, then my rating goes up a little bit, and yours goes down. Over years of play in many matches and tournaments, a small subset of chess players will achieve titles like "grandmaster." Many of these individuals have been studied, and it turns out that they're nothing like what you might expect.

The common stereotype of the chess grandmaster is someone who possesses very high intelligence and an incredible memory. They are thought to play chess well because they can see dozens of moves ahead into a game. (They might also be thought of as obsessive and antisocial, but those parts of the stereotype aren't relevant for our purposes.) When researchers began to study chess grandmasters in the 1940s, they discovered that these people often have average intelligence, and normal memory for everything but chess. They also don't have some master plan for a game consisting of dozens of moves. Because they can't antici-pate every possible countermove by an opponent, it isn't feasible for them to implement such long-term strategies.

However, when these experts' memory skills are tested within the domain of chess, their extraordinary abilities quickly become evident. When briefly presented with a position that had occurred in a real game, chess experts can recreate that position on a second board quickly and accurately, even if that involves the placement of one or two dozen pieces on their respective squares. Novice chess players, as you might expect, perform poorly at this task.[4]

How are the chess experts able to perform such feats? An important part of the story seems to be chunking, or the group-ing of disparate objects into meaningful patterns, as we discussed in the previous chapter. For example, a very common pattern that occurs over and over in chess games is for the king to be placed behind a row of three pawns. The novice chess player would have to remember this by remembering four separate items in working memory. The expert, by contrast, can remember that pattern as a single chunk, which greatly increases his or her working mem-ory capacity. Perhaps most importantly, both chess experts and novices perform poorly when the board to be recreated has been populated by chess pieces placed randomly. In this situation, the chess experts can't rely on chunking to aid them.

Researchers have also tried to estimate how many groupings of pieces a chess expert can recognize instantly. It's thought that the "vocabulary" of the expert is between 50,000 and 100,000 patterns. It's also been estimated that it requires about 10,000 hours of study and practice to acquire this vocabulary. Interest-ingly, this number is consistent with the amount of time required to achieve expertise in a number of disciplines, a finding that has been popularized by Malcolm Gladwell in his book *Outliers*. However, a recent overview of this literature by Brooke Macnamara and colleagues suggests the effects of deliberate practice vary widely by domain.[5]

A belief that deliberate practice is the key has caused some to claim that there really isn't a fundamental difference between experts and nonexperts. Experts are simply individuals who, because of their intense interest and love of a subject, have put in the time necessary to achieve a very high level of performance. Although this conclusion is controversial, it does provide some hope for those of us who wish to acquire expertise. It's heartening to think that expertise is ultimately achievable by virtually anyone.

What's that? You're saying that you don't have 10,000 hours to spare to learn a foreign language? Remember that you don't need to become an expert to achieve a very useful amount of fluency. But you will still need to practice, and research has shed some light on this topic as well.

Before reading any further, we'd like you to participate in a simple experiment. We'd like you to estimate how many classmates' names you can remember from your high school graduating class (first and last names). Perhaps you're thinking that you can name two-thirds of your classmates, or at least half of them. Now take out a sheet of paper, and try to write the names down. Go ahead, we'll wait.

If you actually attempted this experiment, you're probably disappointed at how few names you were able to produce. You were undoubtedly able to immediately scribble down the names of close friends and well-known class personalities, and perhaps a few others. But most people will find that they've created a fairly short list.

This experiment was first conducted by memory researcher Harry Bahrick. He was interested in studying very long-term memory—the things that we remember across decades of our lives. The difficulty with exploring this topic is that most of us don't have extensive records to determine whether our memories are complete or accurate. If we were to ask you what you had for lunch on November 5, 2009, you probably have no way of checking whether you consumed a salad or a sandwich.

Bahrick got around this problem when he realized that almost everyone has detailed records from their late teenage years: their high school yearbooks. He asked a number of individuals to bring their yearbooks to his lab (without looking at them first), and then asked them to carry out tasks like the one you just did: to recall as many of their classmates' names as they could.

If you really did attempt our exercise, then perhaps Bahrick's results won't come as a shock to you. He found that, for an older group of participants who had, on average, graduated from high school forty-eight years earlier, just 6 percent of the total classmates' names were recalled. Intriguingly, however, he found that, for a group who had graduated quite recently (on average, three months earlier), performance wasn't much better: just 15 percent of the classmates' names were recalled.[6]

At one level, this is deeply unsettling. After all, these are the people that we laughed and cried with during a very important part of our lives. But even more than that, the result just doesn't *feel* right: surely we can remember more of our classmates than that. And that intuition is correct. When Bahrick asked his participants to simply *recognize* which of four names belonged to a high school classmate, performance was excellent. For those who had graduated three months earlier, name recognition was 90 percent. And recognition remained at very high levels (80–90 percent) for up to thirty-five years following graduation.

The message to take away from this study is that the assessment of memory depends critically on *how* memory is measured. You really didn't forget your classmate's names: you simply became less able to spontaneously recall them. However, you can still pick out a classmate's name when it is placed with others that are unfamiliar to you.

Bahrick conducted a similar experiment on memory for high school Spanish.[7] Even though participants in this study had a difficult time recalling a Spanish word when given only the English word as a prompt, they could still pick out the correct Spanish word on a multiple choice test. This result occurred for individuals who had studied Spanish up to thirty years prior to the experiment; however, it also depended on how much Spanish they had studied and how well they had performed in the courses. In other words, the longer someone had studied Spanish, and the better their grades had been, the more likely they were to retain the information.[7]

To account for this impressive performance, Bahrick proposed the concept of *permastore* for memories that are extremely durable, resistant to forgetting, and that can last for more than twenty-five years. He suggested that memories acquired over a long period of time are more likely to end up in a permastore state. However, for information to end up in permastore, two conditions must be met.

First, the information must be *overlearned*. For example, Bahrick asked participants to pick out the meaning of the Spanish word *feliz*. They had to choose from among the English words *happy*, *fault*, *feet*, *new*, or *clean*. Because *feliz* is such a common word in Spanish, students were probably exposed to it repeatedly. That is, *feliz* is likely to have been a Spanish word that was overlearned, and therefore, the meaning of *feliz* was less likely to have been forgotten. (*Feliz* means "happy" in case you were wondering.)

Overlearning was first described by Ebbinghaus, and a large body of subsequent research has underscored its importance. So if you are trying to learn vocabulary terms and believe that you've memorized them, you would be well advised to continue reviewing these terms periodically even after you have the subjective impression that you know them. Overlearning will help you to put these words in your permastore.

We have already briefly mentioned the other component that is necessary for permastore, which is distributed practice. Distributed practice means that exposure is spaced out over time. Returning to high school once again, you may recall neglecting the content of a particular course, and then staying up all night to cram for an exam. Although this sort of learning can be effective over the short term, and is better than not studying at all, it seldom leads to the formation of durable memories.[8] For example, if you are going to spend ten hours studying a foreign language over the next week, you'd be much better off studying for ninety minutes a day rather than studying for five hours on two days. Although five hours spent studying over two days is better than not studying at all, it's also not the best use of your time. When it comes to practice and retaining information over a long period of time, just remember: Slow and steady wins the race.

### Take It Personally

Imagine that you're taking part in a psychology experiment. You've been told to read and comprehend target words as they appear, one by one, on a computer screen. You're also asked to answer a question about each of these words. Let's say the word *selfish* appears on the screen, and you are asked "Is the word printed in capital letters?" Obedient participant that you are, you press the "yes" button. Other participants might see *selfish* and be asked, "Does the word rhyme with weight?" (in this case, no), or "Is the word a type of fish?" (again, no). Finally, some participants might be asked, "Does this word describe you?" After responding to a series of such word and question pairs, you are then given a task you weren't expecting. You are asked to recognize as many of the target words as you can.

Do you think the questions you were asked might have an effect on which words you were able to recall? If you have good memory for the previous discussion on levels of processing, the answer would be yes. As you might expect, questions about whether words were printed in capital letters led to relatively poor rates of recognition for those target words. Likewise, questions about whether two words rhymed also resulted in unimpressive performance. As we noted before, in both cases, this is to be expected, because these questions were answered using shallow processing. On the other hand, memory performance was better when participants had to think more deeply about the word (e.g., recognizing that *selfish* is not a type of fish). But the participants best remembered those words when they thought about the words in relation to themselves. This phenomenon is called the *self-reference* effect.[9]

But is the self-reference effect really the result of being asked to consider words in relation just to oneself, or might a similar effect be obtained if the words were related to *any* person? Follow-up research used a self-reference condition like the one we just described, but also employed an "*other*-reference" condition. The idea was to have participants think about the words in relation to a familiar individual, but not someone they person-ally knew. For many of these studies, the go-to other person was Johnny Carson, the talk show host who had appeared on televi-sion every weeknight since the early 1960s. This was someone who would have been instantly recognizable to the participants, but probably not someone they knew very much about. (Car-son, unlike many of today's celebrities, was fairly circumspect.) When the researchers compared the participants' recognition of the trait words in the two conditions, they found that words thought about in relation to oneself were better remembered than the words thought about in relation to Carson. In other words, the effect really is a *self*-reference effect, and not just a consequence of thinking about whether particular traits describe any one person.[10]

The self-reference effect has been explained in several ways, and the arguments tend to be complementary rather than oppos-ing. The first has to do with the *emotional* dimension of the trait words. It probably doesn't matter to you, one way or another, whether Johnny Carson was selfish or incredibly generous. How-ever, when thought about in relation to yourself, the question will engender a variety of emotions (perhaps pride about what a philanthropist you are, or guilty regret that you throw away all those appeals from charity that you receive in the mail).

A second and perhaps more important explanation has to do with the nature of the self. You may now be struggling to learn a foreign language, but you can take some solace from the fol-lowing fact: you are an expert on at least one subject, and that is the story of your life. In fact, you know more about yourself than anyone who has ever lived. Although this may seem a bit narcis-sistic, it is undoubtedly true, and it has important consequences for memory. When we're asked if the word *selfish* describes us, we are able to think about the question by drawing upon *specific* autobiographical memories, such as last week when you treated your colleague to lunch ("See! I'm not selfish!"), or your unwillingness to buy cookies from the Girl Scout who appeared at your door last month ("Well, maybe I am, a little bit"). In the case of Johnny Carson, you probably aren't able to recall specific episodes of generosity or stinginess. Researchers have described the self as "a well-developed and often-used construct." In fact, the self-reference effect is so strong that we are more likely to remember the birthdays of others if those birthdays fall close to our own.[11]

It's possible to profit from the self-reference effect in a variety of ways. So the news here is good indeed. By attempting to learn a foreign language later in life, you can draw upon your extensive life experiences as rich retrieval cues for committing to memory the elements of a second language. Of course, not all concepts you need to remember lend themselves easily to self-reference. But thinking deep thoughts is much better overall than processing information shallowly. When you can use it, self-reference will be there as one of the arrows in your cognitive quiver.

### Emotional Aspects of Memory

It probably comes as no surprise that the ability to learn a new language is affected by one's mood and emotional state. Cognitive scientists have studied the links between memory, mood, and emotion. This section explores how to create an emotional environment that will facilitate pleasurable and effective foreign language learning.

## Think Positive

In exploring the link between thinking and feeling, one basic tenet to keep in mind is that positive information is processed more efficiently and is remembered better and longer than negative information. The superiority of positive over negative information has been shown repeatedly in a wide range of studies, including ones that looked at memory for vocabulary words, grammatical structures, and the content of dialogue and text. This bias toward positive information may be of particular importance (and perhaps relief) to the adult learner because it has also been shown that unpleasant memories weaken over time. Margaret Matlin and David Stang called the overall trend for cognitive systems to favor positive information the *Pollyanna principle*, named after the little girl who in the popular books and movies focuses on the bright side of life in even the most depressing circumstances.[12]

Of course, it would be impossible to achieve any level of mastery in a language by studying only positive vocabulary words or by producing only affirmative sentences. However, because positive linguistic features are easier to process, remember, and recall than negative ones, when it comes to doing things with the language—such as telling a story, making a presentation, or engaging in conversation—you will give yourself an advantage if you approach these activities from a positive standpoint. For example, it will be easier for you to create in your target language a sentence like "The president is a woman" than it will be to create the sentence "The president is not a man." It will also be easier for your audience to understand what you are trying to say, since listeners also process positive information more easily than negative information.

## Be Specific

When Richard was a student, he would study for tests in the same classroom and the same seat where he learned the material and where he would later take the test (nerd alert!). Before a test, he would go to the classroom at night and write his notes on the blackboard. Then he would sit in his seat and study the board, so that on the day of the test, if he had trouble remembering something, he could visualize what he had written on the board in hopes of recalling the information. What Richard was trying to do, without knowing it at the time, was to take advantage of a cognitive phenomenon called *encoding specificity*.

Encoding specificity refers to the fact that memory improves when the context in which you learned material (the encoding) matches the context in which you are asked to remember the material.[13] Conversely, when these contexts do not match, memory ability can suffer. Perhaps this has happened to you. You may have found that you are great at remembering vocabulary words in the classroom and can pass a test with ease. But as soon as you try to apply these words in a real-life setting, they seem to vanish into thin air. When this happens, don't blame your age: blame encoding specificity. The problem arises when there is a mismatch between where and how you learned the words and where and how you want to use them.

Keep in mind too that context does not only mean your external surroundings. Although many studies have measured encoding specificity by manipulating external features like where the material is learned, other characteristics such as one's internal affective state are also susceptible to encoding specificity. For example, people who learn a list of words when they have been drinking do better on recall after drinking again than when they are sober. Also, some veterans of the Gulf War exhibit more negative symptoms of PTSD (post-traumatic stress disorder) near the anniversary of the their initial traumatic event.[14]

One's mood also influences the ability to recall information. In general, memory improves if the mood when the material was learned matches the mood when the material was recalled.[15] For example, when you are angry it's easier to remember other events or situations that also made you angry. Such mood-dependent memories may be one reason why during an argument a person brings up prior anger-inducing events—even if they have nothing to do with the situation at hand.

Mood-dependent learning would predict that being calm and relaxed in class, but anxious and worried during an exam, will lead to impaired test performance. We don't recommend that you make yourself anxious and worried in class. Rather, if you end up recalling the information better in class than on a test, keep in mind that it's a not a reflection of your age or overall cognitive ability, but merely a consequence of encoding specificity. It's normal and happens to people of all ages, so don't become discouraged!

Of course, it's impossible to study information in every possible context and mood in order to avoid memory lapses due to encoding specificity or mood-dependence. However, there are several things that adult language learners can do to make encoding specificity work for them, or at least to lessen its influence. One method would be to learn the language in a way that is as close as possible to how you will eventually use it.

For example, at one point when Richard was studying Portuguese, he was living in Iceland. He went to Brazil for a month of intensive study and then returned to Iceland where he took a telephone test in Portuguese. He failed it. But since he was a cognitive scientist, he thought about what had gone wrong and was determined to try again. So he returned to Brazil for a second round of studying, but this time he tried to match the internal and external encoding context with what he knew he would have to do during the phone test. He even spoke to his Portuguese teacher by phone to practice. He took the phone test again—this time while he was still in Brazil—and passed, which enabled him to join the Foreign Service. Not surprisingly, however, when he took the language test in person (which is required to make sure that the person who takes the phone test is the same person who shows up at work), he did not score as well—since of course the live test was contextually quite different, and he was not proficient enough to be free of context effects. He did score high enough, however, so that the testers knew he hadn't been cheating.

**Be Expansive**
Although encoding specificity is real—even for native speakers—most of us strive for a level of linguistic proficiency that is not so heavily dependent on context. To do this, it is important to vary where, when, and how we learn and study a language. In other words, to lessen the impact of encoding specificity, take advantage of the distributed practice effect. If you have two hours to study, it is better to study for one hour, then take a break by doing something completely different, and then come back and study the material again. Although distributed practice is specific to time, we suggest that you should study the material again in different contexts as well. That doesn't mean to study your notes at home and then study your notes in the library. Rather, you might want to study your notes for an hour, then meet a native speaker with whom you can practice the words you've just been studying in a conversation.

Keep in mind that with distributed practice, each time you return to the material, you will do worse than you had been doing when you left off previously. Not only is this normal, but it is exactly what you want to happen. That's because the goal of distributed practice is to give yourself the opportunity to forget and then relearn the material at a new time. Since relearning is faster than learning, each time you forget something and then relearn it, you reinforce the material in a slightly different way. If you vary the place where you relearn the material as well, you will lessen the specificity of the previous encoding, allowing you to use the language more fluidly in a variety of situations.

Not only that, but taking time away from your studies will allow what are called *incubation* effects to occur. That is, stepping back from a task has been shown, paradoxically, to lead to better problem solving and creativity. Evidence also suggests that even sleep and dreaming promote incubation effects. And not to put too fine a point on it, but don't forget the phenomenon of release from proactive interference mentioned earlier.[16]

So what's the bottom line? Relax. Be sure to study, but when you find yourself getting confused or no longer improving, stop. Do something else—anything else. You might even want to sleep on it. When you come back to the material, you may be surprised at how much you actually remember.

### A Little Knowledge Is a Dangerous, Yet Helpful, Thing

Adult language learners possess an array of highly organized knowledge structures that can serve to aid memory in a top-down, conceptually driven way. By the same token, it is important to recognize that preexisting knowledge structures can create expectations that could be problematic. Consider what happened to Roger.

Famished and exhausted, Roger had just arrived at his destination: a small city in eastern Switzerland. It was his first trip to Europe as an adult, and after two long flights and a journey by train, his top priority was finding something to eat. He entered the first restaurant he found, and waited impatiently to be seated. After a while, it became apparent that he was being ignored. He began to pace back and forth a bit, and tried to make himself as conspicuous as possible. Then he realized he wasn't being ignored any longer. The wait staff of the restaurant had gathered at the back. They were eyeing him with some concern, and holding an animated discussion. Finally, one of the servers approached him, and asked, with some degree of trepidation, "What do you want?" Amazed by this question, Roger blurted out "I want to eat!" Now it was the server's turn to be astonished. "If you want to eat, then sit down!" Roger meekly followed her instruction, and was soon enjoying his meal.

Later in his visit, he picked out a couple of books at a bookstore. He took his selections to the cashier, who proceeded to ring them up. After totaling the price, she looked at him expectantly. He, in turn, looked expectantly back at her. After a moment, it became clear that both of them were waiting for the other to do *something*. With barely controlled exasperation, she informed Roger of the total price—the same amount clearly visible to him on the front of the cash register. She spoke to him slowly, loudly, and distinctly, the way you might address a not-so-bright child. Chastened, he paid for his purchases and beat a hasty retreat.

Before Roger began this trip, he had been feeling rather smug about his ability to cope with the rigors of foreign travel. Unlike the stereotypical "ugly American," who expects everyone to speak English, his knowledge of German was serviceable, and he had made a point of practicing the language well in advance of his trip. He had memorized the requisite tourist expressions in his phrasebook. He had read the relevant sections in a couple of guidebooks for the region. In short, he felt well prepared for interacting with the locals. His subsequent difficulties with tasks as basic as restaurant dining and book buying, therefore, were more than a little disconcerting.

So, what was the cause of Roger's problems? Could he blame jet lag, or the unaccustomed altitude, or the Swiss work force? As you may have guessed by now, his difficulties arose because of a mismatch between Roger's expectations and the expectations of the servers and cashier. The confusion at the restaurant was the result of his experience dining in the United States. Almost invariably, patrons are greeted by a server, or a prominent sign will instruct them to "Please seat yourself" or "Please wait to be seated." In Switzerland, however, no guidance is required, because everyone knows that they should seat themselves. Roger's confusion at the bookstore stemmed from having previously made countless purchases in which the local sales tax was added to the sale price to arrive at a final total. This tax varies by state and even from city to city in the United States, so no one tries to calculate it in advance—you simply wait to be informed of the grand total. In Switzerland, however, taxes are already included in the sale price, so the steps he was waiting for—the addition of the sales tax, and then the announcement of the total—would not occur. Despite his best efforts, Roger had become what he had fervently hoped to avoid: a clueless American abroad.

Roger's training as a cognitive scientist (and perhaps his wounded pride) led him to reflect on these experiences, and to think about them from the perspective of his Swiss hosts. In hindsight, it was apparent why his behavior had mystified the wait staff at the restaurant. In their eyes, he clearly wasn't there to eat, because if he had been, he would have sat down. He didn't seem to be waiting for anyone else—he never glanced at his watch or back at the entrance, for example. And his impatience and pacing only unnerved them further. In a similar way, the cashier at the bookstore couldn't figure out what he was waiting for: the amount that he was required to pay was displayed in large numbers just a few inches from his eyes.

Psychologists have a name for such mismatching expectations: they're called *script errors*. A script is one's mental checklist for events and the order in which they occur. For Americans, the "dining at a restaurant" script would include at least fourteen steps:

1.  Enter the restaurant.
2.  Seat oneself or wait to be seated (as indicated).
3.  Receive menus from the server, and place drink orders.
4.  Decide on what food to order.
5.  Wait.
6.  Give the food order to the server.
7.  Wait.
8.  Food is prepared and brought to the table by the server.
9.  Eat the food.
10. Wait.
11. Receive the check and pay for the food and tip.
12. Wait.
13. Receive the receipt from the server.
14. Exit the restaurant.

This is all blindingly obvious, right? And yet, we're also aware of the subtle and not-so-subtle variations that exist for this script.

At a fast food restaurant, for example, one can jump directly from step 1 to step 6, and the food must be paid for *before* it is consumed. Tipping is not expected, unless there is a very prominent tip jar on the counter. And if someone took a seat at a McDonald's and waited to be served, they would probably end up waiting for a very long time. At many diners and Chinese restaurants in the United States, there is another deviation from the standard script: the check is brought to the table, but the patron must then take it to the counter in order to pay.

So Roger's difficulty at the Swiss restaurant was caused by his assumption that the choice point at step 2 of his dining script was universal. The Swiss wait staff can shoulder some of the blame as well—they were apparently unaware that in *their* restaurant script, step 2 (Always seat yourself)—is *not* universal.

We all possess many, many scripts (also called *schemata*) for actions that we engage in repeatedly. These scripts form part of what psychologists refer to as *semantic memory*, or our general world knowledge. Scripts and schemata are mental frameworks that are based on our shared cultural experiences. As such, they form part of the common ground we use when we communicate. Scripts enable the quick and effortless processing of information, but as Roger's experiences in Switzerland demonstrate, adhering too closely to a script can be dangerous.[17]

These concepts were first investigated by the British experimental psychologist Frederic Bartlett. His research during the 1920s convinced him that the act of remembering involved reconstructing a previous experience, based on the information that is easily retrieved. Any gaps in this retrieval are filled in with inferences based on our existing schemata.[18]

Bartlett came to these conclusions by studying the recall of stories he gave to participants who were undergraduates at

Cambridge University. He made a point of using narratives drawn from less familiar cultures in an attempt to see this "gap filling" process at work. In his most well-known research, he used a Native American legend called "The War of the Ghosts." From a British perspective, the story involves many hard–to-understand elements: it's not clear, for example, whether the aforementioned war is fought with the living or with the dead. It also includes many details that would have been part of the Native Americans' schemata, but not that of Bartlett's participants. For example, the story contains reference to two boys engaged in seal catching, and paddling in canoes. When asked to recall this story at a later time, many participants reported that the boys had been fishing, or had been in boats.

According to Bartlett's reasoning, although his participants were unable to remember exactly what the boys had been up to, they could vaguely remember that they had been standing at the water's edge. They were doing *something*, but they couldn't remember what it was. What *would* one do at the edge of a river? Using their schematic knowledge, the participants filled in the gap by "remembering" that the boys had been fishing.

Just like the Cambridge undergraduates, it's possible that when you are learning a new language (which includes the culture), you may rely on a script or schema from your native language to fill in the gaps. For example, Americans end most of their casual conversations with the phrase "Have a nice day," which is part of the US script for closing a conversation. When Americans study a foreign language they often want to learn how to say, "Have a nice day" even though to end a conversation this way is odd in many other cultures. However, for an American, stopping a conversation after "thank you" or "you're welcome" can feel like something is missing. To fill in the gap the American may look for an alternative phrase that, although not strictly needed in the target language, does not sound odd and will give the American the sense of closure they expect because of their script.

## The Art of Memory

The Roman orator Cicero tells the story of Simonides of Ceos who narrowly escaped a gruesome death. The Greek lyric poet, who lived in the fifth century BC, had offended Scopas, a nobleman of Thessaly, by composing a victory ode that was not to his liking. Scopas was irritated by the inclusion of an extended decorative passage concerning the mythological twins Castor and Pollux. While dining in a banquet hall with Scopas, Simonides was suddenly summoned outside by two young men. At that moment, the roof of the dining hall collapsed, and Scopas and a number of his relatives were killed. In addition, the summoning visitors were nowhere to be found. According to legend, the two young men were said to be—you guessed it—Castor and Pollux, who saved Simonides's life in gratitude for their inclusion in his poem.

When the hall was excavated, it was discovered that the bodies of the dinner guests had been crushed beyond recognition, making it impossible to identify the remains for burial. Simonides was summoned and asked if he could help. He was able to figure out who was who by remembering where the various guests had been seated around the table before he left the building.[19] Recognizing the utility of this technique as an aid to remembering, Simonides is said to have gone on to develop the memory aid now referred to as the *method of loci* (*loci* is the plural of the Latin word *locus*, meaning "place" or "location").

It is also sometimes referred to as the *Memory Palace technique* or the *memory theater*. No matter what it is called, the idea is the same: a familiar location or route is used as a cue to remember a list of items in a specific order. This technique exemplifies one of the major themes of this book: you can take advantage of what you already know to learn something new, such as vocabulary in your target language.

Imagine that you want to remember to buy bagels, milk, and eggs for tomorrow's breakfast. In your mind's eye, you can "drive" a familiar route, such as your daily commute to the office, to help you remember your grocery list. As you pass familiar landmarks, you can associate them with the items you need to buy. If your route takes you past a church with a tall steeple, for example, you could imagine a gigantic bagel speared by the church's spire. If your commute includes driving past a tall apartment building, you could imagine milk running down the building's sides and forming puddles on the ground. And the eggs can be remembered by making use of the golf course near the end of your commute. Just form a mental picture of a gigantic egg cracking down the middle, and disgorging golfers onto the links. When you enter the grocery store, all you'll have to do is hop in your mental vehicle and drive to work. As you pass the church, apartment tower, and golf course, you'll "see" the items on your list.

Of course, in this example, it's not important that you remember the grocery list in a particular order. However, the technique can be used in this way, because in your mental commute you always drive by the church first, then the apartment building, and finally the golf course. Throughout antiquity, Greek and Roman orators used the method to remember the points to be made in a speech in their proper order. There are a number of other techniques besides the method of loci to aid in remembering. Collectively, such mental manipulations are also referred to as *mnemonic devices*, and we'll briefly describe several additional examples, although there are many others.[20]

The method of loci is helpful because all you need to do is associate the items to be remembered with something you already know (a familiar route). But if you're willing to learn a simple poem, you can acquire another powerful memory technique:

One is run,

two is shoe,

three is tree,

four is door

and so on ...

This is the *peg system*, in which words that rhyme with or sound like the cardinal numbers are used like the route in the method of loci. (This poem has many variations—the truncated version shown here is the one that Roger was taught as a young child by his father.)

Now let's go back to the shopping list. With *one is run*, imagine a horse racing along a racetrack, but instead of carrying a jockey, there's an enormous bagel in the saddle. For *two is shoe*, imagine milk in one's shoes, or perhaps leaking out of them with every step. For three, the item to be remembered can take the place of branches or leaves on a tree. So to finish off this three-item grocery list, imagine an egg tree, with brightly colored Easter eggs taking the place of leaves. The exact form of the mental imagery doesn't really matter. All that's needed is for the cue (now tied to a number—something you already know) to connect to the items you want to remember.

Of course, most of the time, you don't need to link a concept to a number. Instead, you probably just want to connect a vocabulary word in your target language to a word or concept in your native language. Using vivid imagery to associate two words is known as the *keyword mnemonic*. Here's an example of how it works. The German word for door is *Tür*. To remember this word, a student who is knowledgeable about the self-reference effect might draw upon an episode in her life as a memory cue. Say she was visiting Istanbul and found herself locked out of her hotel room, made doubly unfortunate by the fact that she had an urgent need to use the room's facilities. Her despair at being blocked by the unyielding *door* in *Tur*key will help her remember the word *Tür* in German (except for the umlaut—those cost extra).

Chances are, you've made use of other mnemonic devices to learn a variety of material. Many children are taught the made-up name *Roy G. Biv*, which is an acronym for remembering the seven colors of the spectrum in their proper sequence (red, orange, yellow, green, blue, indigo, violet). In a similar way, sentences like *My very educated mother just served us nine pies* can be an aid in remembering the order of the planets, with the first letter of each word serving as a cue for remembering Mercury, Venus, Earth, and so on (although with the demotion of Pluto, new sentences have been created with only eight words). Need to remember the eight bones of the wrist? Just recall *Some lovers try positions that they can't handle* to remember scaphoid, lunate, triquetrum, pisiform, trapezium, trapezoid, capitate, hamate. We think of *Spring forward, fall back* to remember how to adjust our clocks, and the rhyme *Thirty days hath September* to figure out whether next week will include April 31 (hint: it probably won't).

That all sounds great, but can such mental manipulations help you learn a foreign language? The answer is yes and no.

Some material does lend itself readily to the use of mnemonic devices, such as in the above examples. Rhymes are easier to remember than prose because words with similar sounds possess an added component to aid in recall, in much the same way that vocal melodies are better remembered than instrumental melodies. Likewise, in the case of the method of loci, the peg system, and the keyword mnemonic, the use of imagery may help jog memory. Interestingly, the method of loci has also been used to treat depression by helping individuals recall positive, self-affirming personal memories.[21]

Unfortunately, mnemonic devices also have some limitations. First of all, the majority of linguistic information to be mastered cannot be adapted easily to these techniques. For example, vivid mental images, no matter how apt or bizarre, will be useful in only a limited number of situations, and may fade quickly unless reinforced through testing. Moreover, words that are associated with a visual image are sometimes confused upon recall (Was the word for door in German *Tür* or was it *Türk*?). Finally, creating images and associations takes time that might be better spent on other learning strategies.[22]

Therefore, our advice is to try to use mnemonic devices only if they feel natural to you and suit the material. Incorporated along with the other strategies we've discussed in this book, mnemonic devices can be looked upon as additional tools in your cognitive tool kit. Mix and match as needed. Keep in mind, however, that learning can't occur unless you also maintain a healthy physical condition and a positive emotional state. If you want to improve your memory ability, be sure to get enough sleep, keep yourself healthy, stay relaxed, and maintain a positive attitude toward your target language and culture.[23]

# Epilogue

Although you have reached the end of this book, we hope this is just the beginning of your foreign language journey. We will have achieved our goal if you now think about language learning as being well within your reach. By letting your life experiences enrich your language learning, your language learning will in turn enrich your life. It's been true for us, and we hope it will be true for you.

# Notes

## 1   Terms and Conditions

1.   The notes in this book contain references to scientific research that supports the claims we put forward. If you don't care about sources, feel free to simply ignore the notes.

2.   On adults learning language more easily than children, see David P. Ausubel, "Adults versus Children in Second-Language Learning: Psychological Considerations," *Modern Language Journal* 48 (7) (1964): 420–424; Stefka H. Marinova-Todd, D. Bradford Marshall, and Catherine E. Snow, "Three Misconceptions about Age and L2 Learning," *TESOL Quarterly* 34 (1) (2000): 9–34; and Mary Schleppegrell, "The Older Language Learner" (Washington, DC: ERIC Clearinghouse on Languages and Linguistics, 1987), http://files.eric.ed.gov/fulltext/ED287313.pdf. On children's ability to acquire a native accent, see Stephen D. Krashen, Michael A. Long, and Robin C. Scarcella, "Age, Rate, and Eventual Attainment in Second Language Acquisition," *TESOL Quarterly* 13 (4) (1979): 573–582. On adults' ability of achieving native-like fluency, see David Birdsong, "Ultimate Attainment in Second Language Acquisition," *Language* 68 (4) (1992): 706–755. On children's having no language learning anxiety, see David P. Ausubel, *Educational Psychology: A Cognitive View* (New York: Holt, Rinehart & Winston, 1968); Gregory K. Moffatt, *The Parenting Journey: From Conception through the Teen Years*

(Santa Barbara, CA: Greenwood, 2004); Schleppegrell, "The Older Language Learner."

3.    On disciplines involved in cognitive science, see Howard Gardner, *The Mind's New Science: A History of the Cognitive Revolution* (New York: Basic Books, 1985).

4.    On top-down processing in reading comprehension, see, e.g., Arthur C. Graesser, Cheryl Bowers, Ute J. Bayen, and Xiangen Hu, "Who Said What? Who Knows What? Tracking Speakers and Knowledge in Narratives," in *New Perspectives on Narrative Perspective*, ed. Willie van Peer and Seymour Chatman, 255–272 (Albany, NY: State University of New York Press, 2001).

5.    On adults' abilities to capitalize on their extensive world knowledge and experience, see, e.g., John B. Black and Robert Wilensky, "An Evaluation of Story Grammars," *Cognitive Science* 3 (3) (1979): 213–230.

6.    On metacognitive and metamemory abilities not being fully developed until adulthood, see Wolfgang Schneider and Kathrin Lockl, "The Development of Metacognitive Knowledge in Children and Adolescents," in *Applied Metacognition*, ed. Timothy J. Perfect and Bennett L. Schwartz, 224–260 (Cambridge: Cambridge University Press, 2002).

7.    On adults' sophisticated understanding of their cognitive processes, see Ethan Zell and Zlatan Krizan, "Do People Have Insight into Their Abilities? A Metasynthesis," *Perspectives on Psychological Science* 9 (2) (2014): 111–125.

8.    On politeness routines learned in childhood, see Jean Berko Gleason, Rivka Y. Perlmann, and Esther Blank Greif, "What's the Magic Word: Learning Language through Politeness Routines," *Discourse Processes* 7 (4) (1984): 493–502.

## 2   Set Yourself Up for Success

1.    On the availability heuristic, see Amos Tversky and Daniel Kahneman, "Availability: A Heuristic for Judging Frequency and Probability,"

*Cognitive Psychology* 5 (2) (1973): 207–232. For the use of heuristics in artificial intelligence, see, e.g., Herbert A. Simon, "The Structure of Ill-Structured Problems," *Artificial Intelligence* 4 (1973): 181–201, http://www.public.iastate.edu/~cschan/235/6_Simon_Ill_defined_problem .pdf.

2. On how likely people are to buy earthquake insurance as the memory of the earthquake fades, see Riccardo Rebonato, *Plight of the Fortune Tellers: Why We Need to Manage Financial Risk Differently* (Princeton, NJ: Princeton University Press, 2010).

3. On the planning fallacy, see Roger Buehler, Dale Griffin, and Michael Ross, "Exploring the 'Planning Fallacy:' Why People Underestimate Their Task Completion Times," *Journal of Personality and Social Psychology* 67 (3) (1994): 366–381; Daniel Kahneman and Amos Tversky, "Intuitive Prediction: Biases and Corrective Procedures," Technical Report PTR-1042-77-6, 1977, http://www.dtic.mil/cgi-bin/GetTRDoc?AD=ADA0 47747.

4. On the benefits of process-focused planning, see Shelley E. Taylor, Lien B. Pham, Inna D. Rivkin, and David A. Armor, "Harnessing the Imagination: Mental Simulation, Self-Regulation, and Coping," *American Psychologist* 53 (4) (1998): 429–439.

5. On counterfactual thinking, see Victoria Husted Medvec, Scott F. Madey, and Thomas Gilovich, "When Less Is More: Counterfactual Thinking and Satisfaction among Olympic Medalists," *Journal of Personality and Social Psychology* 69 (4) (1995): 603–610.

6. On the benefits on maintaining positive beliefs about aging, see Becca R. Levy, Alan B. Zonderman, Martin D. Slade, and Luigi Ferrucci, "Age Stereotypes Held Earlier in Life Predict Cardiovascular Events in Later Life," *Psychological Science* 20 (3) (2009): 296–298.

7. For more on the hindsight bias, see Neal J. Roese and Kathleen D. Vohs, "Hindsight Bias," *Perspectives on Psychological Science* 7 (5) (2012): 411–426.

8. On the time it takes to form new habits, in addition to Maxwell Maltz, *Psycho-Cybernetics: A New Way to Get More Living Out of Life* (New York: Prentice Hall, 1960), see, e.g., Phillippa Lally, Cornelia H. M. Van

Jaarsveld, Henry W. W. Potts, and Jane Wardle, "How Are Habits Formed: Modeling Habit Formation in the Real World," *European Journal of Social Psychology* 40 (6) (2010): 998–1009.

9.   On predictors of how successful people are at giving up smoking, see Andrew Hyland, Ron Borland, Qiang Li, Hua H. Yong, Ann McNeill, Geoffrey T. Fong, Richard J. O'Connor, and K. M. Cummings, "Individual-Level Predictors of Cessation Behaviours among Participants in the International Tobacco Control (ITC) Four Country Survey," *Tobacco Control 15* (Suppl. III) (2006): iii83–iii94.

10.   On distributed versus massed practice (or cramming), see John Dunlosky, Katherine A. Rawson, Elizabeth J. Marsh, Mitchell J. Nathan, and Daniel T. Willingham, "Improving Students' Learning with Effective Learning Techniques: Promising Directions from Cognitive and Educational Psychology," *Psychological Science in the Public Interest* 14 (1) (2013): 4–58.

11.   "Specific, high (hard) goals lead to a higher level of task performance": Edwin A. Locke and Gary P. Latham, "New Directions in Goal-Setting Theory," *Current Directions in Psychological Science* 15 (5) (2006): 265–268, at 265.

12.   For Bandura's work on self-efficacy, see Albert Bandura, "Self-Efficacy: Toward a Unifying Theory of Behavioral Change," *Psychological review* 84 (2) (1977): 191–215.

13.   On negative experiences leading to low self-efficacy, see Madeline E. Ehrman, *Understanding Second Language Learning Difficulties* (Thousand Oaks, CA: Sage, 1996).

14.   For Navratilova's interviews, see Giles Smith, "Tennis: Wimbledon '93: Navratilova Looking Forward to a Happy 21st: The Woman with More Titles Than Any Other Player Relishes the Unpredictability of Grass, Especially on Centre Court," *Independent*, June 21, 1993, http://www.independent.co.uk/sport/tennis-wimbledon-93-navratilova-looking-forward-to-a-happy-21st-the-woman-with-more-titles-than-any-other-player-relishes-the-unpredictability-of-grass-especially-on-centre-court-giles-smith-reports-1492895.html. For more on self-handicapping, see

Arthur Frankel and Mel L. Snyder, "Egotism among the Depressed: When Self-Protection Becomes Self-Handicapping," 1987, paper presented at the annual convention of the American Psychological Association, http:// files.eric.ed.gov/fulltext/ED289120.pdf.

15. On self-handicapping becoming a way of life, see, e.g., S. Berglas and E. E. Jones, "Control of Attributions about the Self through Self-handicapping Strategies: The Appeal of Alcohol and the Role of Underachievement," *Personality and Social Psychology Bulletin* 4 (2) (1978): 200–206.

16. On lessening anxiety about trying to achieve proficiency later in life, see Zoltán Dörnyei, "Motivation and Motivating in the Foreign Language Classroom," *Modern Language Journal* 78 (3) (1994): 273–284, and "Motivation in Second and Foreign Language Learning," *Language Teaching* 31 (3) (1998): 117–135.

17. On Vygotsky's concept of zone of proximal development, see Lev S. Vygotsky, *Mind in Society: The Development of Higher Psychological Processes* (Cambridge, MA: Harvard University Press, 1980).

18. On the ability to gauge for yourself whether you're "in the zone," see Janet Metcalfe, "Metacognitive Judgments and Control of Study," *Current Directions in Psychological Science* 18 (3) (2009): 159–163.

## 3  Aspects of Language

1. On the nature of English spelling–sound relationships and George Bernard Shaw, see Ben Zimmer, "GHOTI," *New York Times Magazine*, June 25, 2010, http://www.nytimes.com/2010/06/27/magazine/27FOB -onlanguage-t.html?_r=0 Zimmer 2010.

2. On the advice to focus solely on speaking and listening so as not to be confused by irregularities, see, e.g., Paul Pimsleur, *How to Learn a Foreign Language* (New York: Simon & Schuster, 2013).

3. Focusing on spoken material "deprives the older learner of his principal learning tool": Ausubel, "Adults versus Children in Second-Language Learning," 423.

4.   For these statistics and more, see Office of the Inspector General, "Inspection of the Foreign Service Institute," March 31, 2013, http://oig .state.gov/system/files/209366.pdf.

5.   On the various definitions of *fluency*, see Marie-Noëlle Guillot, *Fluency and Its Teaching* (Clevedon: Multilingual Matters, 1999).

6.   For more on aphasia, see http://www.aphasia.org.

7. For Crawford's story, see Philip Crawford, "Bon Appétit? Not So Fast," *New York Times*, May 6, 2014, http://www.nytimes.com/2014/05/07/ opinion/bon-appetit-not-so-fast.html.

8.   For more on interlanguages, see Larry Selinker, "Interlanguage," *International Review of Applied Linguistics* 10 (1–4) (1972): 209–231.

9.   For more on fossilization, see, e.g., Larry Selinker and John T. Lamendella, "The Role of Extrinsic Feedback in Interlanguage Fossilization," *Language Learning* 29 (2) (1979): 363–376.

10.   On the cognitive science notion of common ground, see Herbert H. Clark and C. R. Marshall, "Definite Reference and Mutual Knowledge," in *Elements of Discourse Understanding*, ed. Aravind K. Joshi, Bonnie L. Webber, and Ivan A. Sag, 10–63 (Cambridge: Cambridge University Press, 1981).

## 4   Pragmatics and Culture

1.   On adults' ability to learn vocabulary and grammar and how it compares to that of children, see, e.g., Ellen Bialystok and Kenji Hakuta, *In Other Words: The Science and Psychology of Second-Language Acquisition* (New York: Basic Books, 1994); James Emil Flege, Grace H. Yeni-Komshian, and Serena Liu, "Age Constraints on Second-Language Acquisition," *Journal of Memory and Language* 41 (1) (1999): 78–104.

2.   For more on the ILR Speaking Skill Scale, see http://www.govtilr. org/skills/ILRscale2.htm.

3.   "Make your conversational contribution such as is required": H. Paul Grice, "Logic and Conversation," in *Syntax and Semantics*, vol. 3:

*Speech Acts*, ed. Peter Cole and Jerry. L. Morgan, 41–58, at 45 (New York: Academic Press, 1975). For more on Grice's Cooperative Principle and his conversational maxims, see also Grice, "Further Notes on Logic and Conversation," in *Syntax and Semantics*, vol. 9: *Pragmatics*, ed. Peter Cole, 183–197 (New York: Academic Press, 1978).

4.  For examples of when we might no longer assume a conversational partner is cooperating, see Richard Roberts and Roger Kreuz, "Nonstandard Discourse and Its Coherence," *Discourse Processes* 16 (4) (1993): 451–464.

5.  For more on Austin's speech act theory, see John L. Austin, *How to Do Things with Words*, 2nd ed. ed. J. O. Urmson and Marina Sbisá (Cambridge, MA: Harvard University Press, 1975).

6.  On figurative speech as fundamental to language, see Howard R. Pollio, Jack M. Barlow, Harold J. Fine, and Marilyn R. Pollio, *Psychology and the Poetics of Growth: Figurative Language in Psychology, Psychotherapy, and Education* (Hillsdale, NJ: Erlbaum, 1977).

7.  On ambiguous figurative language not being rare, again see Pollio et al., *Psychology and the Poetics of Growth*. On the shared root of the English *to be* and the Sanskrit to *breathe*, see Julian Jaynes, *The Origin of Consciousness in the Breakdown of the Bicameral Mind* (Boston: Houghton Mifflin, 1976).

8.  For estimates on how many different figures of speech there are, see, e.g., Alex Preminger, and T. V. F. Brogan, eds., *The New Princeton Encyclopedia of Poetry and Poetics* (New York: MJF Books, 1993). On Americans as greatly prone to exaggeration, see, e.g., "American Exaggerations," *New York Times*, August 4, 1854, p. 4, http://times machine.nytimes.com/timesmachine/1854/08/04/88135952.html. For Queen Elizabeth II's famously understated remark, see Caroline Davies, "How the Royal Family Bounced Back from Its 'Annus Horribilis,'" *Guardian*, May 24, 2012, http://www.theguardian.com/uk/2012/may/24/royal-family-bounced-back-annus-horribilis.

9.  On how metaphors become less malleable over time, see Anne Cutler, "Idioms: The Colder the Older," *Linguistic Inquiry* 13 (1982):

317–320. On the novelty of an idiomatic expression upon one's first encounter with it, see Jeannette Littlemore, "Metaphoric Intelligence and Foreign Language Learning," *Humanising Language Teaching* 3 (2) (2001), http://www.hltmag.co.uk/mar01/mart1.htm.

10. On metaphoric intelligence, see Littlemore, "Metaphoric Intelligence and Foreign Language Learning."

11. On using language to maintain interpersonal relationships, see Gabriele Kasper, *Can Pragmatic Competence Be Taught?* (Honolulu: University of Hawai'i, Second Language Teaching & Curriculum Center, 1997), http://www.nflrc.hawaii.edu/NetWorks/NW06/.

12. On the difficulty of translating interpersonal abilities between cultures, see, e.g., Raymond Carroll, *Cultural Misunderstandings: The French-American Experience* (University of Chicago Press, 1988). On high-context versus low-context cultures, see Edward T. Hall, *Beyond Culture* (New York: Anchor Books, 1976).

13. On Japan, China, and Korea as high-context cultures, see, e.g., Elizabeth Würtz, "Intercultural Communication on Websites: A Cross-Cultural Analysis of Websites from High-Context Cultures and Low-Context Cultures," *Journal of Computer-Mediated Communication* 11 (1) (2006): 274–299. On leaving things unsaid in high-context cultures, see again Hall, *Beyond Culture*.

14. On Germany, Norway, and the United States as low-context cultures, see again Würtz, "Intercultural Communication on Websites." On schizophrenics and their partners' common ground, see Roberts and Kreuz, "Nonstandard Discourse and Its Coherence."

15. On people in Turkey as more extroverted than people in Japan, see C. Ashley Fulmer, Michele J. Gelfand, Arie W. Kruglanski, Chu Kim-Prieto, Ed Diener, Antonio Pierro, and E. Tory Higgins, "On "Feeling Right" in Cultural Contexts: How Person-Culture Match Affects Self-Esteem and Subjective Well-Being," *Psychological Science* 21 (11) (2010): 1563–1569.

16. On taking into account your own unique relationship to the language and culture you want to learn, see Kasper, *Can Pragmatic Competence Be Taught?*

17.   On the uncanny valley, see M. Mori, "The Uncanny Valley," *IEEE Robotics and Automation Magazine* 19 (2) (1970): 98–100.

## 5   Language and Perception

1.   On Salthouse's general slowing hypothesis, see Timothy A. Salthouse, "The Processing-Speed Theory of Adult Age Differences in Cognition," *Psychological Review* 103 (3) (1996): 403–428.

2.   On the pauses in conversations between native speakers, see Susan Ervin-Tripp, "Children's Verbal Turn-Taking," in *Developmental Pragmatics*, ed. Elinor Ochs and Bambi Schieffelin, 391–414 (New York: Academic Press, 1979). On the extensive cognitive processing that goes into such pauses, see Willem J. M. Levelt, *Speaking: From Intention to Articulation* (Cambridge, MA: MIT Press, 1989).

3.   On the "filled pause," see Geoffrey Beattie, "The Dynamics of Interruption and the Filled Pause," *British Journal of Social and Clinical Psychology* 16 (3) (1977): 283–284.

4.   On the efficacy of "train your brain" practices at improving other abilities, see Adrian M. Owen, Adam Hampshire, Jessica A. Grahn, Robert Stenton, Said Dajani, Alistair S. Burns, Robert J. Howard, and Clive G. Ballard, "Putting Brain Training to the Test," *Nature* 465 (2010): 775–778.

5.   For research on bilinguals regarding the cognitive benefits of foreign language learning, see Ellen Bialystok, Fergus I. M. Craik, David W. Green, and Tamar H. Gollan, "Bilingual Minds," *Psychological Science in the Public Interest* 10 (3) (2009): 89–129.

6.   For estimates on the relative numbers of monolinguals, bilinguals, and multilinguals, see G. Richard Tucker, "A Global Perspective on Bilingualism and Bilingual Education," Center for Applied Linguistics, 1999, http://www.cal.org/resource-center/briefs-digests/digests.

7.   For research on the cognitive abilities of those who can speak more than one language, see Bialystok et al., "Bilingual Minds." For research on the performance of bilinguals on tests of selective attention and

multitasking, see Ellen Bialystok and Fergus I. M. Craik, "Cognitive and Linguistic Processing in the Bilingual Mind," *Current Directions in Psychological Science* 19 (1) (2010): 19–23. On bilinguals' performance on the Stroop Test, see Ellen Bialystok, "Reshaping the Mind: The Benefits of Bilingualism," *Canadian Journal of Experimental Psychology* 65 (4) (2011): 229–235.

8.    For the explanation of bilinguals being better at multitasking in terms of inhibiting one language, see Ellen Bialystok, Fergus I. M. Craik, and Gigi Luk, "Bilingualism: Consequences for Mind and Brain," *Trends in Cognitive Sciences* 16 (4) (2012): 240–250. For bilinguals' superior performance on concept formation tasks, following complex instructions, and switching to new instructions, see Ellen Bialystok and Michelle M. Martin, "Attention and Inhibition in Bilingual Children: Evidence from the Dimensional Change Card Sort Task," *Developmental Science* 7 (3) (2004): 325–339; Elizabeth Peal and Wallace C. Lambert, "The Relations of Bilingualism to Intelligence," *Psychological Monographs: General and Applied* 76 (27) (1962): 1–23. On the cognitive and linguistic advantages of bilingualism outweighing negative aspects, see Bialystok and Craik, "Cognitive and Linguistic Processing in the Bilingual Mind."

9.    For the details of the research into the incidence of Alzheimer's in bilinguals compared to monolinguals, see Ellen Bialystok, Fergus I. M. Craik, and Morris Freedman, "Bilingualism as a Protection against the Onset of Symptoms of Dementia," *Neuropsychologia* 45 (2) (2007): 459–464.

10.    For the details of the study in India on the incidence of Alzheimer's in bilinguals, see Suvarna Alladi, Thomas H. Bak, Vasanta Duggirala, Bapiraju Surampudi, Mekala Shailaja, Anuj Kumar Shukla, Jaydip Ray Chaudhuri, and Subhash Kaul, "Bilingualism Delays Age at Onset of Dementia, Independent of Education and Immigration Status," *Neurology* 81 (22) (2013): 1938–1944. For the positive effects of bilingualism even when the person acquired the language in adulthood, see Thomas H. Bak, Jack J. Nissan, Michael M. Allerhand, and Ian J. Deary, "Does Bilingualism Influence Cognitive Aging?" *Annals of Neurology* 75 (6) (2014): 959–963. For the suggestion that the positive benefits of bilingualism only accrue to those who use both languages all

the time, see Claudia Dreifus, "The Bilingual Advantage," *New York Times*, May 30, 2011, http://www.nytimes.com/2011/05/31/science/31conversation.html.

11. On the claim that further research is needed to determine what caused the differences in age of onset between monolinguals and bilinguals, see Judith F. Kroll, "The Consequences of Bilingualism for the Mind and the Brain," *Psychological Science in the Public Interest* 10 (3) (2009): i–ii.

12. On the issue of whether being socially active prevents dementia, or whether people who don't have dementia are more likely to be socially active, see Hui-Xin Wang, Anita Karp, Bengt Winblad, and Laura Fratiglioni, "Late-Life Engagement in Social and Leisure Activities Is Associated with a Decreased Risk of Dementia: A Longitudinal Study from the Kungsholmen Project," *American Journal of Epidemiology* 155 (12) (2002): 1081–1087.

13. On the spontaneous rate of speech in English and Japanese, see Harry Osser and Frederick Peng, "A Cross Cultural Study of Speech Rate," *Language and Speech* 7 (2) (1964): 120–125.

14. For research on the phenomenon of generalization and transfer, see, e.g., Ann R. Bradlow and Tessa Bent, "Perceptual Adaptation to Non-Native Speech," *Cognition* 106 (2) (2008): 707–729.

15. For research into the generalization effect, see Cynthia G. Clopper and David B. Pisoni, "Some Acoustic Cues for the Perceptual Categorization of American English Regional Dialects," *Journal of Phonetics* 32 (1) (2004): 111–140.

16. For the details of Flege and his colleagues' study on age constraints on second-language learning, see James Emil Flege, Grace H. Yeni-Komshian, and Serena Liu, "Age Constraints on Second-Language Acquisition," *Journal of Memory and Language* 41 (1) (1999): 78–104.

17. For details on the research on Italians who immigrated to the United States, see Ian R. A. Mackay, James E. Flege, and Satomi Imai, "Evaluating the Effects of Chronological Age and Sentence Duration on

Degree of Perceived Foreign Accent," *Applied Psycholinguistics* 27 (2) (2006): 157–183.

18. For the quote from Meryl Streep, see Benjamin Wood, "The Iron Lady: Meryl Streep Says Accents Are the Easiest Thing She Does," *Entertainment Weekly*, December 7, 2011, http://insidemovies.ew.com/2011/12/07/meryl-streep-iron-lady-panel/.

## 6   Cognition from Top to Bottom

1.   On the McGurk effect, see Harry McGurk and John MacDonald, "Hearing Lips and Seeing Voices," *Nature* 264 (1976): 746–748.

2.   For Lin's Unspeakableness project, see http://uniquelang.peiyinglin.net.

3.   On the question of the extent to which language influences thought, see, e.g., Benjamin Lee Whorf and Stuart Chase, *Language, Thought, and Reality: Selected Writings of Benjamin Lee Whorf*, ed. John B. Carroll (Cambridge, MA: MIT Press, 1956). On treating concepts from the native language as prototypes for concepts in the new language, see Gilbert A. Jarvis, "Psychological Processes in Foreign and Second Language Learning," in *Critical Issues in Foreign Language Instruction*, ed. Ellen S. Silber, 29–42, Garland Reference Library of Social Science, Volume 459 (New York: Routledge, 1991).

4.   On the topic of how thinking in a native or a foreign language influences problem solving, see Boaz Keysar, Sayuri L. Hayakawa, and Sun Gyu An, "The Foreign-Language Effect: Thinking in a Foreign Tongue Reduces Decision Biases," *Psychological Science* 23 (6) (2012): 661–668. On speaking a nonnative language giving the speaker distance from a moral problem, see Boaz Keysar and Albert Costa, "Our Moral Tongue," *New York Times*, June 20, 2014, http://www.nytimes.com/2014/06/22/opinion/sunday/moral-judgments-depend-on-what-language-we-are-speaking.html. On using one's native language versus a nonnative language to remember autobiographical events and its effect on the arousal of emotion, see Viorica Marian and Margarita

Kaushanskaya, "Self-Construal and Emotion in Bicultural Bilinguals," *Journal of Memory and Language* 51 (2) (2004): 190–201.

5.    For the estimate that a native college-educated speaker of English knows only about 17,000 words, see Eugene B. Zechmeister, Andrea M. Chronis, William L. Cull, Catherine A. D'Anna, and Noreen A. Healy, "Growth of a Functionally Important Lexicon," *Journal of Literacy Research* 27 (2) (1995): 201–212.

6.    On the use of idiolect to determine the identity of the Unabomber, see James R. Fitzgerald, "Using a Forensic Linguistic Approach to Track the Unabomber," in *Profilers: Leading Investigators Take You Inside the Criminal Mind*, ed. John H. Campbell, 193–222 (Amherst, NY: Prometheus Books, 2010); on its use to identify the authors of the *Federalist Papers*, see Frederick Mosteller and David L. Wallace, "Inference in an Authorship Problem: A Comparative Study of Discrimination Methods Applied to the Authorship of the Disputed Federalist Papers," *Journal of the American Statistical Association* 58, (302) (1963): 275–309; and on its use to identify the author of *Primary Colors*, see Donald W. Foster, *Author Unknown: On the Trail of Anonymous* (New York: Henry Holt, 2000).

7.    For Ogden's proposal of Basic English, see Charles Kay Ogden, *Basic English: A General Introduction with Rules and Grammar* (London: Paul Treber, 1944).

8.    On using the word order from your native language in your target language as an instance of negative transfer, see David N. Perkins and Gavriel Salomon, "Transfer of Learning," in *The International Encyclopedia of Education*, 2nd ed., vol. 11, ed. Torsten Husen and T. Neville Postlethwaite, 6452–6457 (Oxford: Pergamon Press, 1992).

9.    On high-road and low-road transfer as the two mechanisms adult language learners can use to facilitate positive transfer, see Gavriel Salomon and David N. Perkins, "Rocky Roads to Transfer: Rethinking Mechanisms of a Neglected Phenomenon," *Educational Psychologist* 24 (2) (1989): 113–142. On the example of driving a rental truck after driving a car as one of low-road transfer, see Perkins and Salomon, "Transfer of Learning."

10. For these examples of metaphors, see George Lakoff and Mark Johnson, *Metaphors We Live By* (Chicago: University of Chicago Press, 1980), 44–45.

11. For research on expressions of heartbreak, see Kathrin Abe, Nadja Kesper, and Matthias Warich, "Domain Mappings—General Results," in *Cross-Cultural Metaphors: Investigating Domain Mappings across Cultures*, ed. Marcus Callies and Rüdiger Zimmerman, 29–40 (Marburg: Philipps-Universität, 2002).

12. For his work on idioms, see Raymond W. Gibbs, Jr., *The Poetics of Mind: Figurative Thought, Language, and Understanding* (Cambridge: Cambridge University Press, 1994); these examples come from p. 9.

13. On thinking about the conceptual mappings of metaphors and idioms in your target language as an aid to organization and learning, see, e.g., Andrew Ortony, "Why Metaphors Are Necessary and Not Just Nice," *Educational Theory* 25 (1) (1975): 45–53; Hugh G. Petrie and Rebecca S. Oshlag, "Metaphor and Learning," in *Metaphor and Thought*, 2nd ed., ed. Andrew Ortony, 579–609 (Cambridge: Cambridge University Press, 1993).

## 7 Making Memories …

1. For Miller's "the magical number seven, plus or minus two," see George A. Miller, "The Magical Number Seven, Plus or Minus Two: Some Limits on our Capacity for Processing Information," *Psychological Review* 63 (2) (1956): 81–97.

2. On the steady decline of memory span after the age of twenty, see Jacques Grégoire and Martial Van der Linden, "Effect of Age on Forward and Backward Digit Spans," *Aging, Neuropsychology, and Cognition* 4 (2) (1997): 140–149.

3. "The adult learns best not by rote …": Schleppegrell, "The Older Language Learner," 3.

4. For research on the exact size of working memory, see Nelson Cowan, *Working Memory Capacity* (New York: Taylor & Francis, 2004);

Jonathan E. Thiele, Michael S. Pratte, and Jeffrey N. Rouder, "On Perfect Working-Memory Performance with Large Numbers of Items," *Psychonomic Bulletin and Review* 18 (5) (2011): 958–963.

5. For Alan Baddeley's research on working memory, see Alan D. Baddeley and Graham Hitch, "Working Memory," *Psychology of Learning and Motivation* 8 (1974): 47–89.

6. For research on the decline in middle age of the central executive's ability to deal with competing information, see Elizabeth L. Glisky, "Changes in Cognitive Function in Human Aging," in *Brain Aging: Models, Methods, and Mechanisms*, ed. David R. Riddle, 3–20 (Boca Raton, FL: Taylor & Francis, 2007); Lynn Hasher, Rose T. Zacks, and Cynthia P. May, "Inhibitory Control, Circadian Arousal, and Age," in *Attention and Performance XVII: Cognitive Regulation of Performance: Interaction of Theory and Application*, ed. Daniel Gopher and Asher Koriat, 653–675 (Cambridge, MA: MIT Press, 1999).

7. On the claim that the efficacy of the central executive reaches its peak during one's twenties, see Cinzia R. De Luca and Richard J. Leventer, "Developmental Trajectories of Executive Functions Across the Lifespan," in *Executive Functions and the Frontal Lobes: A Lifespan Perspective*, vol. 3, ed. Vicki Anderson, Rani Jacobs, and Peter J. Anderson, 23–56 (New York: Psychology Press, 2008). For the claim that it does not peak as much as previously thought, see Paul Verhaeghen, "Aging and Executive Control: Reports of a Demise Greatly Exaggerated," *Current Directions in Psychological Science* 20 (3) (2011): 174–180.

8. For the claim that our ability to multitask is not as great as we think and declines over time, see Hironori Ohsugi et al., "Differences in Dual-Task Performance and Prefrontal Cortex Activation between Younger and Older Adults,"*BMC Neuroscience* 14 (10) (2013), http://www .biomedcentral.com/1471-2202/14/10; Christopher Chabris and Daniel Simons, *The Invisible Gorilla: And Other Ways Our Intuitions Deceive Us* (New York: Crown, 2010).

9. For more on depth of processing and Craik and Tulving's classic experiment, see Fergus I. M. Craik and Robert S. Lockhart, "Levels of Processing: A Framework for Memory Research," *Journal of Verbal*

*Learning and Verbal Behavior* 11 (6) (1972): 671–684; Fergus I. M. Craik and Endel Tulving, "Depth of Processing and the Retention of Words in Episodic Memory," *Journal of Experimental Psychology: General* 104 (3) (1975): 268–294.

10. For a critical view of the depth of processing approach, see, e.g., Alan D. Baddeley, "The Trouble with Levels: A Reexamination of Craik and Lockhart's Framework for Memory Research," *Psychological review* 85 (3) (1978): 139–152.

11. "The most important single factor influencing learning": David P. Ausubel, *Educational Psychology: A Cognitive View* (New York: Holt, Rinehart & Winston, 1968), vi.

12. For Ebbinghaus's proposal of a third way of measuring memory, see Hermann Ebbinghaus, *Memory: A Contribution to Experimental Psychology* (1885; New York: Dover, 1964).

13. For Squire and Slater's study of the ability to recognize names of TV programs and racehorses, see Larry R. Squire and Pamela C. Slater, "Forgetting in Very Long-Term Memory as Assessed by an Improved Questionnaire Technique," *Journal of Experimental Psychology: Human Learning and Memory* 1 (1) (1975): 50–54.

14. For the claim that recognition memory can be excellent many decades after learning, see Harry P. Bahrick, "Semantic Memory Content in Permastore: Fifty Years of Memory for Spanish Learned in School," *Journal of Experimental Psychology: General* 113 (1) (1984): 1–29.

15. On the kanji for fortune telling, see James W. Heisig, *Remembering the Kanji: A Complete Course on How Not to Forget the Meaning and Writing of Japanese Characters* (Honolulu: University of Hawai'i Press, 2011), 32.

16. For the Yerkes–Dodson law, see Robert M. Yerkes and John D. Dodson, "The Relation of Strength of Stimulus to Rapidity of Habit-Formation," *Journal of Comparative Neurology and Psychology* 18 (1908): 459–482.

17. For the claim that how someone responds to additional cognitive demands placed on a task depends on the task itself, the cognitive

strategy used, and the level of mastery, see Janina A. Hoffmann, Bettina von Helversen, and Jörg Rieskamp, "Deliberation's Blindsight: How Cognitive Load Can Improve Judgments," *Psychological Science* 24 (6) (2013): 869–879.

18. For the claim that even routine tasks can require extra mental processing, see Jean-François Bonnefon, Aidan Feeney, and Wim De Neys, "The Risk of Polite Misunderstandings," *Current Directions in Psychological Science* 20 (5) (2011): 321–324.

19. For more on proactive interference, see Robert G. Crowder, *Principles of Learning and Memory* (Hillsdale, NJ: Erlbaum, 1976).

20. For the details of this study on proactive interference, see Lisa Emery, Sandra Hale, and Joel Myerson, "Age Differences in Proactive Interference, Working Memory, and Abstract Reasoning," *Psychology and Aging* 23 (3) (2008): 634–645.

## 8 ... And Making Memories Work for You

1. The TOT state is a "mild torment, something like the brink of a sneeze": Roger Brown and David McNeill, "The 'Tip of the Tongue' Phenomenon," *Journal of Verbal Learning and Verbal Behavior* 5 (4) (1966): 325–337, at 326.

2. For more on TOT states, see Donna J. Dahlgren, "Impact of Knowledge and Age on Tip-of-the-Tongue Rates," *Experimental Aging Research* 24 (2) (1998): 139–153; Marilyn K. Heine, Beth A. Ober, and Gregory K. Shenaut, "Naturally Occurring and Experimentally Induced Tip-of-the-Tongue Experiences in Three Adult Age Groups," *Psychology and Aging* 14 (3) (1999): 445–457.

3. For more on TOT states and aging, see Timothy A. Salthouse and Arielle R. Mandell, "Do Age-Related Increases in Tip-of-the-Tongue Experiences Signify Episodic Memory Impairments?" *Psychological Science* 24 (12) (2013): 2489–2497.

4.    For the claim that novice chess players perform poorly on the task of recreating a position, see William G. Chase and Herbert A. Simon, "Perception in Chess," *Cognitive Psychology* 4 (1) (1973): 55–81.

5.    For the claim that the vocabulary of the chess expert is between 50,000 and 100,000 patterns, see Herbert A. Simon and Kevin Gilmartin, "A Simulation of Memory for Chess Positions," *Cognitive Psychology* 5 (1) (1973): 29–46. For the estimate of 10,000 hours of practice to acquire the vocabulary in chess and other disciplines, see K. Anders Ericsson, Ralf T. Krampe, and Clemens Tesch-Römer, "The Role of Deliberate Practice in the Acquisition of Expert Performance," *Psychological Review* 100 (3) (1993): 363–406, and Malcolm Gladwell, *Outliers: The Story of Success* (London: Penguin UK, 2008). For the claim that the effects of practice vary widely by domain, see Brooke N. Macnamara, David Z. Hambrick, and Frederick L. Oswald, "Deliberate Practice and Performance in Music, Games, Sports, Education, and Professions: A Meta-Analysis," *Psychological Science* 25 (8) (2014): 1608–1618.

6.    For Bahrick's results on recall of classmates' names, see Harry P. Bahrick, Phyllis O. Bahrick, and Roy P. Wittlinger, "Fifty Years of Memory for Names and Faces: A Cross-Sectional Approach," *Journal of Experimental Psychology: General* 104 (1) (1975): 54–75.

7.    For Bahrick's experiment on memory for high school Spanish, see Bahrick, "Semantic Memory Content in Permastore."

8.    For more on learning techniques, see John Dunlosky, Katherine A. Rawson, Elizabeth J. Marsh, Mitchell J. Nathan, and Daniel T. Willingham, "Improving Students' Learning with Effective Learning Techniques: Promising Directions from Cognitive and Educational Psychology," *Psychological Science in the Public Interest* 14 (1) (2013): 4–58.

9.    For the self-reference effect, see Timothy B. Rogers, Nicholas A. Kuiper, and William S. Kirker, "Self-Reference and the Encoding of Personal Information," *Journal of Personality and Social Psychology* 35 (9) (1977): 677–688.

10.    For the claim that the self-reference effect really is a *self*-reference effect, see Charles Lord, "Schemas and Images as Memory Aids: Two

Modes of Processing Social Information," *Journal of Personality and Social Psychology* 38 (2) (1980): 257–269, and Lord, "Imagining Self and Others: Reply to Brown, Keenan, and Potts," *Journal of Personality and Social Psychology* 53 (3) (1987): 445–450.

11. For the claim that the self is "a well-developed and often-used construct," see Cynthia S. Symons and Blair T. Johnson, "The Self-Reference Effect in Memory: A Meta-Analysis," *Psychological Bulletin* 121 (3) (1997): 371–394, at 371. For the claim that people are more likely to remember the birthdays of others if those birthdays fall close to their own, see Selin Kesebir and Shigehiro Oishi, "A Spontaneous Self-Reference Effect in Memory: Why Some Birthdays Are Harder to Remember Than Others," *Psychological Science* 21 (10) (2010): 1525–1531.

12. For the claim that unpleasant memories weaken over time, see W. Richard Walker, John J. Skowronski, and Charles P. Thompson, "Life is Pleasant—And Memory Helps to Keep It That Way!" *Review of General Psychology* 7 (2) (2003): 203–210. For the Pollyanna principle, see Margaret Matlin and David Stang, *The Pollyanna Principle: Selectivity in Language, Memory, and Thought* (Cambridge, MA: Schenkman, 1978).

13. For more on encoding specificity, see Endel Tulving and Donald M. Thomson, "Encoding Specificity and Retrieval Processes in Episodic Memory," *Psychological Review* 80 (5) (1973): 352–373.

14. For a study that measures encoding specificity by manipulating external features, see Duncan R. Godden and Alan D. Baddeley, "Context-Dependent Memory in Two Natural Environments: On Land and Underwater," *British Journal of Psychology* 66 (3) (1975): 325–331. For the claim that one's affective state is also susceptible to encoding specificity, see John D. Teasdale and Sarah J. Fogarty, "Differential Effects of Induced Mood on Retrieval of Pleasant and Unpleasant Events from Episodic Memory," *Journal of Abnormal Psychology* 88 (3) (1979): 248–257. For the claim that people do better recalling words after drinking if they've learned the words while drinking, see Herbert Weingartner, Wolansa Adefris, James E. Eich, and Dennis L. Murphy, "Encoding-Imagery Specificity in Alcohol State-Dependent Learning,"

*Journal of Experimental Psychology: Human Learning and Memory* 2 (1) (1976): 83–87. For veterans of the Gulf War exhibiting more negative PTSD symptoms near the anniversary of the traumatic event, see Charles A. Morgan, Susan Hill, Patrick Fox, Peter Kingham, and Steven M. Southwick, "Anniversary Reactions in Gulf War Veterans: A Follow-up Inquiry 6 Years After the War," *American Journal of Psychiatry* 156 (7) (1999): 1075–1079.

15. For the claim that memory improves if the mood when the material was learned matches the mood when the material was recalled, see Paul H. Blaney, "Affect and Memory: A Review," *Psychological Bulletin* 99 (2) (1986): 229–246.

16. For the claim that stepping back from a task can lead to better problem solving and creativity, see, e.g., Steven M. Smith, Thomas B. Ward, and Ronald A. Finke, eds., *The Creative Cognition Approach* (Cambridge, MA: MIT Press, 1995). For evidence that sleep and dreaming promote incubation effects, see, e.g., Deirdre Barrett, "'The Committee of Sleep': A Study of Dream Incubation for Problem Solving," *Dreaming* 3 (2) (1993): 115–122.

17. For more on scripts or schemata and semantic memory, see Roger C. Schank and Robert P. Abelson, *Scripts, Plans, Goals, and Understanding: An Inquiry into Human Knowledge Structures* (Hillsdale, NJ: Erlbaum, 1977).

18. For Bartlett's research on semantic memory, see Frederic C. Bartlett, *Remembering: A Study in Experimental and Social Psychology* (1932; Cambridge: Cambridge University Press,1995).

19. For more on Cicero's story of Simonides of Ceos, see E. W. Sutton and H. Rackham, *Cicero: On the Orator, Books I–II* (Cambridge, MA: Harvard University Press, 1942).

20. For more on mnemonic devices, see Douglas J. Herrmann, Michael M. Gruneberg, and Douglas Raybeck, *Improving Memory and Study Skills: Advances in Theory and Practice* (Toronto: Hogrefe & Huber, 2002).

21. For the claim that rhymes are easier to remember than prose, see Michael W. Weiss, Sandra E. Trehub, and E. Glenn Schellenberg,

"Something in the Way She Sings: Enhanced Memory for Vocal Melodies," *Psychological Science* 23 (10) (2012): 1074–1078. On the method of loci being used to treat depression, see Tim Dalgleish, Lauren Navrady, Elinor Bird, Emma Hill, Barnaby D. Dunn, and Ann-Marie Golden, "Method-of-Loci as a Mnemonic Device to Facilitate Access to Self-Affirming Personal Memories for Individuals with Depression," *Clinical Psychological Science* 1 (2) (2013): 156–162.

22. For the claim that vivid mental images will only be useful in limited situations, see Russell N. Carney and Joel R. Levin, "Do Mnemonic Memories Fade as Time Goes By? Here's Looking Anew!" *Contemporary Educational Psychology* 23 (3) (1998): 276–297; Margaret H. Thomas and Alvin Y. Wang, "Learning by the Keyword Mnemonic: Looking for Long-Term Benefits," *Journal of Experimental Psychology: Applied* 2 (4) (1996): 330–342. For the idea that creating images and associations takes time away from other learning strategies, see Dunlosky et al., "Improving Students' Learning; Herrmann et al., *Improving Memory and Study Skills*.

23. On the importance of staying healthy for improving your memory, see Herrmann et al., *Improving Memory and Study Skills*.

# Suggestions for Further Reading

Brown, Alan S. 2012. *The Tip of the Tongue State*. New York: Psychology Press.

If you'd like to know more about interference and tip-of-the tongue states, Brown's book provides a comprehensive and up-to-date survey of research on this topic.

Brown, Peter, Henry L. Roediger, and Mark A. McDaniel. 2014. *Make It Stick: The Science of Successful Learning*. Cambridge, MA: Harvard University Press.

This book provides more information about many of the memory phenomena and mnemonic devices that are mentioned in chapters 7 and 8.

Chabris, Christopher, and Daniel Simons. 2011. *The Invisible Gorilla: And Other Ways Our Intuitions Deceive Us*. New York: Crown.

Among other fascinating topics, Chabris and Simons take a critical look at the claims for "brain training" that we mention in chapter 5.

Herrmann, Douglas J., Michael M. Gruneberg, and Douglas Raybeck. 2002. *Improving Memory and Study Skills: Advances in Theory and Practice*. Toronto: Hogrefe & Huber.

This is a great book that takes a holistic approach to understanding and using mnemonic devices in order to improve study skills.

Leaver, Betty Lou, Madeline Ehrman, and Boris Shekhtman. 2005. *Achieving Success in Second Language Acquisition*. Cambridge: Cambridge University Press, 2005.

This very useful book addresses cognition and learning strategies, especially as they apply to the undergraduate student.

Marcus, Gary. 2012. *Guitar Zero: The Science of Becoming Musical at Any Age*. London: Penguin Books.

There are important similarities between learning a foreign language in adulthood and learning to play a musical instrument. Marcus's book is an account of his quest for proficiency at guitar playing.

Wyner, Gabriel. 2014. *Fluent Forever: How to Learn Any Language Fast and Never Forget It*. New York: Harmony Books.

There are many books that take more of a "how to" approach to learning a second language; Wyner's book is a good place to start. His approach makes use of visual imagery and spaced practice to master vocabulary and grammar.

# References

Abe, Kathrin, Nadja Kesper, and Matthias Warich. 2002. Domain mappings—general results. In *Cross-Cultural Metaphors: Investigating Domain Mappings across Cultures*, ed. Marcus Callies and Rüdiger Zimmerman, 29–40. Marburg: Philipps-Universität.

Alladi, Suvarna, Thomas H. Bak, Vasanta Duggirala, Bapiraju Surampudi, Mekala Shailaja, Anuj Kumar Shukla, Jaydip Ray Chaudhuri, and Subhash Kaul. 2013. Bilingualism delays age at onset of dementia, independent of education, and immigration status. *Neurology* 81 (22): 1938–1944.

American Exaggerations. 1854. *New York Times*, August 4, p. 4. http://timesmachine.nytimes.com/timesmachine/1854/08/04/88135952.html.

Austin, John L. 1975. *How to Do Things with Words*, 2nd ed., ed. J. O. Urmson and Marina Sbisá. Cambridge, MA: Harvard University Press.

Ausubel, David P. 1964. Adults versus children in second-language learning: Psychological considerations. *Modern Language Journal* 48 (7): 420–424.

Ausubel, David P. 1968. *Educational Psychology: A Cognitive View*. New York: Holt, Rinehart & Winston.

Baddeley, Alan D. 1978. The trouble with levels: A reexamination of Craik and Lockhart's framework for memory research. *Psychological Review* 85 (3): 139–152.

Baddeley, Alan D., and Graham Hitch. 1974. Working memory. *Psychology of Learning and Motivation* 8: 47–89.

Bahrick, Harry P. 1984. Semantic memory content in permastore: Fifty years of memory for Spanish learned in school. *Journal of Experimental Psychology: General* 113 (1): 1–29.

Bahrick, Harry P., Phyllis O. Bahrick, and Roy P. Wittlinger. 1975. Fifty years of memory for names and faces: A cross-sectional approach. *Journal of Experimental Psychology: General* 104 (1): 54–75.

Bak, Thomas H., Jack J. Nissan, Michael M. Allerhand, and Ian J. Deary. 2014. Does bilingualism influence cognitive aging? *Annals of Neurology* 75 (6): 959–963.

Bandura, Albert. 1977. Self-efficacy: Toward a unifying theory of behavioral change. *Psychological Review* 84 (2): 191–215.

Barrett, Deirdre. 1993. "The Committee of Sleep": A study of dream incubation for problem solving. *Dreaming* 3 (2): 115–122.

Bartlett, Frederic C. (1932) 1995. *Remembering: A Study in Experimental and Social Psychology*. Cambridge: Cambridge University Press.

Beattie, Geoffrey. 1977. The dynamics of interruption and the filled pause. *British Journal of Social and Clinical Psychology* 16 (3): 283–284.

Berglas, S., and E. E. Jones. 1978. Control of attributions about the self through self-handicapping strategies: The appeal of alcohol and the role of underachievement. *Personality and Social Psychology Bulletin* 4 (2): 200–206.

Bialystok, Ellen. 2011. Reshaping the mind: The benefits of bilingualism. *Canadian Journal of Experimental Psychology* 65 (4): 229–235.

Bialystok, Ellen, and Fergus I.M. Craik. 2010. Cognitive and linguistic processing in the bilingual mind. *Current Directions in Psychological Science* 19 (1): 19–23.

Bialystok, Ellen, Fergus I.M. Craik, and Morris Freedman. 2007. Bilingualism as a protection against the onset of symptoms of dementia. *Neuropsychologia* 45 (2): 459–464.

Bialystok, Ellen, Fergus I.M. Craik, David W. Green, and Tamar H. Gollan. 2009. Bilingual minds. *Psychological Science in the Public Interest* 10 (3): 89–129.

Bialystok, Ellen, Fergus I.M. Craik, and Gigi Luk. 2012. Bilingualism: Consequences for mind and brain. *Trends in Cognitive Sciences* 16 (4): 240–250.

Bialystok, Ellen, and Kenji Hakuta. 1994. *In Other Words: The Science and Psychology of Second-Language Acquisition.* New York: Basic Books.

Bialystok, Ellen, and Michelle M. Martin. 2004. Attention and inhibition in bilingual children: Evidence from the dimensional change card sort task. *Developmental Science* 7 (3): 325–339.

Birdsong, David. 1992. Ultimate attainment in second language acquisition. *Language* 68 (4): 706–755.

Black, John B., and Robert Wilensky. 1979. An evaluation of story grammars. *Cognitive Science* 3 (3): 213–230.

Blaney, Paul H. 1986. Affect and memory: A review. *Psychological Bulletin* 99 (2): 229–246.

Bonnefon, Jean-François, Aidan Feeney, and Wim De Neys. 2011. The risk of polite misunderstandings. *Current Directions in Psychological Science* 20 (5): 321–324.

Bradlow, Ann R., and Tessa Bent. 2008. Perceptual adaptation to nonnative speech. *Cognition* 106 (2): 707–729.

Brown, Roger, and David McNeill. 1966. The "tip of the tongue" phenomenon. *Journal of Verbal Learning and Verbal Behavior* 5 (4): 325–337.

Buehler, Roger, Dale Griffin, and Michael Ross. 1994. Exploring the "planning fallacy": Why people underestimate their task completion times. *Journal of Personality and Social Psychology* 67 (3): 366–381.

Carney, Russell N., and Joel R. Levin. 1998. Do mnemonic memories fade as time goes by? Here's looking anew! *Contemporary Educational Psychology* 23 (3): 276–297.

Carroll, Raymonde. 1988. *Cultural Misunderstandings: The French-American Experience*. Chicago: University of Chicago Press.

Chabris, Christopher, and Daniel Simons. 2011. *The Invisible Gorilla: And Other Ways Our Intuitions Deceive Us*. New York: Crown.

Chase, William G., and Herbert A. Simon. 1973. Perception in chess. *Cognitive Psychology* 4 (1): 55–81.

Clark, Herbert H., and C. R. Marshall. 1981. Definite reference and mutual knowledge. In *Elements of Discourse Understanding*, ed. Aravind K. Joshi, Bonnie L. Webber, and Ivan A. Sag, 10–63. Cambridge: Cambridge University Press.

Clopper, Cynthia G., and David B. Pisoni. 2004. Some acoustic cues for the perceptual categorization of American English regional dialects. *Journal of Phonetics* 32 (1): 111–140.

Cowan, Nelson. 2004. *Working Memory Capacity*. New York: Taylor & Francis.

Craik, Fergus I.M., and Robert S. Lockhart. 1972. Levels of processing: A framework for memory research. *Journal of Verbal Learning and Verbal Behavior* 11 (6): 671–684.

Craik, Fergus I.M., and Endel Tulving. 1975. Depth of processing and the retention of words in episodic memory. *Journal of Experimental Psychology: General* 104 (3): 268–294.

Crawford, Philip. 2014. Bon appétit? Not so fast. *New York Times*, May 6. http://www.nytimes.com/2014/05/07/opinion/bon-appetit-not-so-fast.html.

Crowder, Robert G. 1976. *Principles of Learning and Memory*. Hillsdale, NJ: Erlbaum.

Cutler, Anne. 1982. Idioms: The colder the older. *Linguistic Inquiry* 13: 317–320.

Dahlgren, Donna J. 1998. Impact of knowledge and age on tip-of-the-tongue rates. *Experimental Aging Research* 24 (2): 139–153.

Dalgleish, Tim, Lauren Navrady, Elinor Bird, Emma Hill, Barnaby D. Dunn, and Ann-Marie Golden. 2013. Method-of-loci as a mnemonic device to facilitate access to self-affirming personal memories for individuals with depression. *Clinical Psychological Science* 1 (2): 156–162.

Davies, Caroline. 2012. How the royal family bounced back from its "annus horribilis." *Guardian*, May 24. http://www.theguardian.com/uk/2012/may/24/royal-family-bounced-back-annus-horribilis.

De Luca, Cinzia R., and Richard J. Leventer. 2008. Developmental trajectories of executive functions across the lifespan. In *Executive Functions and the Frontal Lobes: A Lifespan Perspective 3*, ed. Vicki Anderson, Rani Jacobs, and Peter J. Anderson, 23–56. New York: Psychology Press.

Dörnyei, Zoltán. 1994. Motivation and motivating in the foreign language classroom. *Modern Language Journal* 78 (3): 273–284.

Dörnyei, Zoltán. 1998. Motivation in second and foreign language learning. *Language Teaching* 31 (3): 117–135.

Dreifus, Claudia. 2011. The bilingual advantage. *New York Times*, May 30. http://www.nytimes.com/2011/05/31/science/31conversation.html.

Dunlosky, John, Katherine A. Rawson, Elizabeth J. Marsh, Mitchell J. Nathan, and Daniel T. Willingham. 2013. Improving students' learning with effective learning techniques: Promising directions from cognitive and educational psychology. *Psychological Science in the Public Interest* 14 (1): 4–58.

Ebbinghaus, Hermann. (1885) 1962. *Memory: A Contribution to Experimental Psychology*. New York: Dover.

Ehrman, Madeline E. 1996. *Understanding Second Language Learning Difficulties*. Thousand Oaks, CA: Sage.

Emery, Lisa, Sandra Hale, and Joel Myerson. 2008. Age differences in proactive interference, working memory, and abstract reasoning. *Psychology and Aging* 23 (3): 634–645.

Ericsson, K. Anders, Ralf T. Krampe, and Clemens Tesch-Römer. 1993. The role of deliberate practice in the acquisition of expert performance. *Psychological Review* 100 (3): 363–406.

Ervin-Tripp, Susan. 1979. Children's verbal turn-taking. In *Developmental Pragmatics*, ed. Elinor Ochs and Bambi Schieffelin, 391–414. New York: Academic Press.

Fitzgerald, James R. 2010. Using a forensic linguistic approach to track the Unabomber. In *Profilers: Leading Investigators Take You Inside the Criminal Mind*, ed. John H. Campbell, 193–222. Amherst, NY: Prometheus Books.

Flege, James Emil, Grace H. Yeni-Komshian, and Serena Liu. 1999. Age constraints on second-language acquisition. *Journal of Memory and Language* 41 (1): 78–104.

Foster, Donald W. 2000. *Author Unknown: On the Trail of Anonymous*. New York: Henry Holt.

Frankel, Arthur, and Mel L. Snyder. 1987. Egotism among the depressed: When self-protection becomes self-handicapping. Paper presented at the annual convention of the American Psychological Association. http://files.eric.ed.gov/fulltext/ED289120.pdf.

Fulmer, C. Ashley, Michele J. Gelfand, Arie W. Kruglanski, Chu Kim-Prieto, Ed Diener, Antonio Pierro, and E. Tory Higgins. 2010. On "feeling right" in cultural contexts: How person-culture match affects self-esteem and subjective well-being. *Psychological Science* 21 (11): 1563–1569.

Gardner, Howard. 1985. *The Mind's New Science: A History of the Cognitive Revolution*. New York: Basic Books.

Gibbs, Raymond W., Jr. 1994. *The Poetics of Mind: Figurative Thought, Language, and Understanding*. Cambridge: Cambridge University Press.

Gladwell, Malcolm. 2008. *Outliers: The Story of Success*. London: Penguin UK.

Gleason, Jean Berko, Rivka Y. Perlmann, and Esther Blank Greif. 1984. What's the magic word: Learning language through politeness routines. *Discourse Processes* 7 (4): 493–502.

Glisky, Elizabeth L. 2007. Changes in cognitive function in human aging. In *Brain Aging: Models, Methods, and Mechanisms*, ed. David R. Riddle, 3–20. Boca Raton, FL: Taylor & Francis.

Godden, Duncan R., and Alan D. Baddeley. 1975. Context-dependent memory in two natural environments: On land and underwater. *British Journal of Psychology* 66 (3): 325–331.

Graesser, Arthur C., Cheryl Bowers, Ute J. Bayen, and Xiangen Hu. 2001. Who said what? Who knows what? Tracking speakers and knowledge in narratives. In *New Perspectives on Narrative Perspective*, ed. Willie van Peer and Seymour Chatman, 255–272. Albany, NY: State University of New York Press.

Grégoire, Jacques, and Martial Van der Linden. 1997. Effect of age on forward and backward digit spans. *Neuropsychology, Development, and Cognition, Section B: Aging, Neuropsychology, and Cognition* 4 (2): 140–149.

Grice, H. Paul 1975. Logic and conversation. In *Syntax and Semantics*, vol. 3: *Speech Acts*, ed. Peter Cole and Jerry. L. Morgan, 41–58. New York: Academic Press.

Grice, H. Paul 1978. Further notes on Logic and Conversation. In *Syntax and Semantics*, vol. 9: *Pragmatics*, ed. Peter Cole, 183–197. New York: Academic Press.

Guillot, Marie-Noëlle. 1999. *Fluency and Its Teaching*. Clevedon: Multilingual Matters.

Hall, Edward. T. 1976. *Beyond Culture*. New York: Anchor Books.

Hasher, Lynn, Rose T. Zacks, and Cynthia P. May. 1999. Inhibitory control, circadian arousal, and age. In *Attention and Performance XVII: Cognitive Regulation of Performance: Interaction of Theory and Application*, ed. Daniel Gopher and Asher Koriat, 653–675. Cambridge, MA: MIT Press.

Heine, Marilyn K., Beth A. Ober, and Gregory K. Shenaut. 1999. Naturally occurring and experimentally induced tip-of-the-tongue experiences in three adult age groups. *Psychology and Aging* 14 (3): 445–457.

Heisig, James W. 2011. *Remembering the Kanji: A Complete Course on how not to Forget the Meaning and Writing of Japanese Characters*. Honolulu: University of Hawai'i Press.

Herrmann, Douglas J., Douglas Raybeck, and Michael M. Gruneberg. 2002. *Improving Memory and Study Skills: Advances in Theory and Practice*. Toronto: Hogrefe & Huber.

Hoffmann, Janina A., Bettina von Helversen, and Jörg Rieskamp. 2013. Deliberation's blindsight: How cognitive load can improve judgments. *Psychological Science* 24 (6): 869–879.

Hyland, Andrew, Ron Borland, Qiang Li, Hua H. Yong, Ann McNeill, Geoffrey T. Fong, Richard J. O'Connor, and K. M. Cummings. 2006. Individual-level predictors of cessation behaviours among participants in the International Tobacco Control (ITC) four country survey. *Tobacco Control* 15 (Suppl. 3): iii83–iii94.

ILR Speaking Skill Scale. Accessed on August 27, 2014. http://www.govtilr.org/skills/ILRscale2.htm.

Jarvis, Gilbert A. 1991. Psychological processes in foreign and second language learning. In *Critical Issues in Foreign Language Instruction*, ed. Ellen S. Silber, 29–42. Garland Reference Library of Social Science, Volume 459. New York: Routledge.

Jaynes, Julian. 1976. *The Origin of Consciousness in the Breakdown of the Bicameral Mind*. Boston: Houghton Mifflin.

Kahneman, Daniel, and Amos Tversky. 1977. Intuitive prediction: Biases and corrective procedures. Technical Report PTR-1042-77-6. http://www.dtic.mil/cgi-bin/GetTRDoc?AD=ADA047747.

Kasper, Gabriele. 1997. *Can Pragmatic Competence Be Taught?* Honolulu: University of Hawai'i, Second Language Teaching & Curriculum Center; http://www.nflrc.hawaii.edu/NetWorks/NW06/.

Kesebir, Selin, and Shigehiro Oishi. 2010. A spontaneous self-reference effect in memory: Why some birthdays are harder to remember than others. *Psychological Science* 21 (10): 1525–1531.

Keysar, Boaz, and Albert Costa. 2014. Our moral tongue. *New York Times*, June 20. http://www.nytimes.com/2014/06/22/opinion/sunday/moral-judgments-depend-on-what-language-we-are-speaking.htm.

Keysar, Boaz, Sayuri L. Hayakawa, and Sun Gyu An. 2012. The foreign-language effect: Thinking in a foreign tongue reduces decision biases. *Psychological Science* 23 (6): 661–668.

Krashen, Stephen D., Michael A. Long, and Robin C. Scarcella. 1979. Age, rate, and eventual attainment in second language acquisition. *TESOL Quarterly* 13 (4): 573–582.

Kroll, Judith F. 2009. The consequences of bilingualism for the mind and the brain. *Psychological Science in the Public Interest* 10 (3): i–ii.

Lakoff, George, and Mark Johnson. 1980. *Metaphors We Live By*. Chicago: University of Chicago Press.

Lally, Phillippa, Cornelia H.M. Van Jaarsveld, Henry W.W. Potts, and Jane Wardle. 2010. How are habits formed: Modeling habit formation in the real world. *European Journal of Social Psychology* 40 (6): 998–1009.

Levelt, Willem J.M. 1989. *Speaking: From Intention to Articulation*. Cambridge, MA: MIT Press.

Levy, Becca R., Alan B. Zonderman, Martin D. Slade, and Luigi Ferrucci. 2009. Age stereotypes held earlier in life predict cardiovascular events in later life. *Psychological Science* 20 (3): 296–298.

Lin, Pei-Ying. Unspeakableness. Accessed on August 26, 2014. http://uniquelang.peiyinglin.net.

Littlemore, Jeannette. 2001. Metaphoric intelligence and foreign language learning. *Humanising Language Teaching* 3 (2). http://www.hltmag.co.uk/mar01/mart1.htm.

Locke, Edwin A., and Gary P. Latham. 2006. New directions in goal-setting theory. *Current Directions in Psychological Science* 15 (5): 265–268.

Lord, Charles G. 1980. Schemas and images as memory aids: Two modes of processing social information. *Journal of Personality and Social Psychology* 38 (2): 257–269.

Lord, Charles G. 1987. Imagining self and others: Reply to Brown, Keenan, and Potts. *Journal of Personality and Social Psychology* 53 (3): 445–450.

Mackay, Ian R.A., James E. Flege, and Satomi Imai. 2006. Evaluating the effects of chronological age and sentence duration on degree of perceived foreign accent. *Applied Psycholinguistics* 27 (2): 157–183.

Macnamara, Brooke N., David Z. Hambrick, and Frederick L. Oswald. 2014. Deliberate practice and performance in music, games, sports, education, and professions: A meta-analysis. *Psychological Science* 25 (8): 1608–1618.

Maltz, Maxwell. 1960. *Psycho-Cybernetics: A New Way to Get More Living Out of Life.* New York: Prentice Hall.

Marian, Viorica, and Margarita Kaushanskaya. 2004. Self-construal and emotion in bicultural bilinguals. *Journal of Memory and Language* 51 (2): 190–201.

Marinova-Todd, Stefka H., D. Bradford Marshall, and Catherine E. Snow. 2000. Three misconceptions about age and L2 learning. *TESOL Quarterly* 34 (1): 9–34.

Matlin, Margaret, and David Stang. 1978. *The Pollyanna Principle: Selectivity in Language, Memory, and Thought.* Cambridge, MA: Schenkman.

McGurk, Harry, and John MacDonald. 1976. Hearing lips and seeing voices. *Nature* 264:746–748.

Medvec, Victoria Husted, Scott F. Madey, and Thomas Gilovich. 1995. When less is more: Counterfactual thinking and satisfaction among Olympic medalists. *Journal of Personality and Social Psychology* 69 (4): 603–610.

Metcalfe, Janet. 2009. Metacognitive judgments and control of study. *Current Directions in Psychological Science* 18 (3): 159–163.

Miller, George A. 1956. The magical number seven, plus or minus two: Some limits on our capacity for processing information. *Psychological Review* 63 (2): 81–97.

Moffatt, Gregory K. 2004. *The Parenting Journey: From Conception through the Teen Years*. Santa Barbara, CA: Greenwood.

Morgan, Charles A., Susan Hill, Patrick Fox, Peter Kingham, and Steven M. Southwick. 1999. Anniversary reactions in Gulf War veterans: A follow-up inquiry 6 years after the war. *American Journal of Psychiatry* 156 (7): 1075–1079.

Mori, M. 1970. The uncanny valley. *IEEE Robotics and Automation Magazine* 19 (2): 98–100.

Mosteller, Frederick, and David L. Wallace. 1963. Inference in an authorship problem: A comparative study of discrimination methods applied to the authorship of the disputed *Federalist Papers*. *Journal of the American Statistical Association* 58 (302): 275–309.

National Aphasia Association. 2014. Accessed on August 25, 2014. http://www.aphasia.org.

Office of the Inspector General. 2013. "Inspection of the Foreign Service Institute." March 31. oig.state.gov/documents/organization/209366.pdf.

Ogden, Charles Kay. 1944. *Basic English: A General Introduction with Rules and Grammar*. London: Paul Treber.

Ohsugi, Hironori, Shohei Ohgi, Kenta Shigemori, and Eric B. Schneider. 2013. Differences in dual-task performance and prefrontal cortex activation between younger and older adults. *BMC Neuroscience* 14 (10). http://www.biomedcentral.com/1471-2202/14/10.

Ortony, Andrew. 1975. Why metaphors are necessary and not just nice. *Educational Theory* 25 (1): 45–53.

Osser, Harry, and Frederick Peng. 1964. A cross cultural study of speech rate. *Language and Speech* 7 (2): 120–125.

Owen, Adrian M., Adam Hampshire, Jessica A. Grahn, Robert Stenton, Said Dajani, Alistair S. Burns, Robert J. Howard, and Clive G. Ballard. 2010. Putting brain training to the test. *Nature* 465:775–778.

Peal, Elizabeth, and Wallace C. Lambert. 1962. The relations of bilingualism to intelligence. *Psychological Monographs* 76 (27): 1–23.

Perkins, David N., and Gavriel Salomon. 1992. Transfer of learning. In *The International Encyclopedia of Education*, 2nd ed., vol. 11, ed. Torsten Husen and T. Neville Postlethwaite, 6452–6457. Oxford: Pergamon Press.

Petrie, Hugh G., and Rebecca S. Oshlag. 1993. Metaphor and learning. In *Metaphor and Thought*, 2nd ed., ed. Andrew Ortony, 579–609. Cambridge: Cambridge University Press.

Pimsleur, Paul. 2013. *How to Learn a Foreign Language*. New York: Simon & Schuster.

Pollio, Howard R., Jack M. Barlow, Harold J. Fine, and Marilyn R. Pollio. 1977. *Psychology and the Poetics of Growth: Figurative Language in Psychology, Psychotherapy and Education*. Hillsdale, NJ: Erlbaum.

Preminger, Alex, and T. V. F. Brogan, eds. 1993. *The New Princeton Encyclopedia of Poetry and Poetics*. New York: MJF Books.

Rebonato, Riccardo. 2010. *Plight of the Fortune Tellers: Why We Need to Manage Financial Risk Differently*. Princeton, NJ: Princeton University Press.

Roberts, Richard M., and Roger J. Kreuz. 1993. Nonstandard discourse and its coherence. *Discourse Processes* 16 (4): 451–464.

Roberts, Richard M., and Roger J. Kreuz. 1994. Why do people use figurative language? *Psychological Science* 5 (3): 159–163.

Roese, Neal J., and Kathleen D. Vohs. 2012. Hindsight bias. *Perspectives on Psychological Science* 7 (5): 411–426.

Rogers, Timothy B., Nicholas A. Kuiper, and William S. Kirker. 1977. Self-reference and the encoding of personal information. *Journal of Personality and Social Psychology* 35 (9): 677–688.

Salomon, Gavriel, and David N. Perkins. 1989. Rocky roads to transfer: Rethinking mechanisms of a neglected phenomenon. *Educational Psychologist* 24 (2): 113–142.

Salthouse, Timothy A. 1996. The processing-speed theory of adult age differences in cognition. *Psychological Review* 103 (3): 403–428.

Salthouse, Timothy A., and Arielle R. Mandell. 2013. Do age-related increases in tip-of-the-tongue experiences signify episodic memory impairments? *Psychological Science* 24 (12): 2489–2497.

Schank, Roger C., and Robert P. Abelson. 1977. *Scripts, Plans, Goals, and Understanding: An Inquiry into Human Knowledge Structures.* Hillsdale, NJ: Erlbaum.

Schleppegrell, Mary. 1987. The older language learner. Washington, DC: ERIC Clearinghouse on Languages and Linguistics. http://files.eric .ed.gov/fulltext/ED287313.pdf.

Schneider, Wolfgang, and Kathrin Lockl. 2002. The development of metacognitive knowledge in children and adolescents. In *Applied Metacognition*, ed. Timothy J. Perfect and Bennett L. Schwartz, 224–260. Cambridge: Cambridge University Press.

Schwartz, Bennett L., and Janet Metcalfe. 2011. Tip-of-the-tongue (TOT) states: Retrieval, behavior, and experience. *Memory and Cognition* 39 (5): 737–749.

Selinker, Larry. 1972. Interlanguage. *International Review of Applied Linguistics* 10 (1–4): 209–231.

Selinker, Larry, and John T. Lamendella. 1979. The role of extrinsic feedback in interlanguage fossilization. *Language Learning* 29 (2): 363–376.

Simon, Herbert A. 1973. The structure of ill-structured problems. *Artificial Intelligence* 4:181–201. http://www.public.iastate.edu/~cschan/235/ 6_Simon_Ill_defined_problem.pdf.

Simon, Herbert A., and Kevin Gilmartin. 1973. A simulation of memory for chess positions. *Cognitive Psychology* 5 (1): 29–46.

Smith, Giles. 1993. Tennis: Wimbledon '93: Navratilova looking forward to a Happy 21st: The woman with more titles than any other player relishes the unpredictability of grass, especially on Centre Court." *Independent*, June 21. http://www.independent.co.uk/sport/tennis-wim

bledon-93-navratilova-looking-forward-to-a-happy-21st-the-woman
-with-more-titles-than-any-other-player-relishes-the-unpredictability-of
-grass-especially-on-centre-court-giles-smith-reports-1492895.html.

Smith, Steven M., Thomas B. Ward, and Ronald A. Finke, eds. 1995. *The Creative Cognition Approach*. Cambridge, MA: MIT Press.

Squire, Larry R., and Pamela C. Slater. 1975. Forgetting in very long-term memory as assessed by an improved questionnaire technique. *Journal of Experimental Psychology: Human Learning and Memory* 1 (1): 50–54.

Sutton, E. W., and H. Rackham. 1942. *Cicero: On the Orator, Books I–II*. Cambridge, MA: Harvard University Press.

Symons, Cynthia S., and Blair T. Johnson. 1997. The self-reference effect in memory: A meta-analysis. *Psychological Bulletin* 121 (3): 371–394.

Taylor, Shelley E., Lien B. Pham, Inna D. Rivkin, and David A. Armor. 1998. Harnessing the imagination: Mental simulation, self-regulation, and coping. *American Psychologist* 53 (4): 429–439.

Teasdale, John D., and Sarah J. Fogarty. 1979. Differential effects of induced mood on retrieval of pleasant and unpleasant events from episodic memory. *Journal of Abnormal Psychology* 88 (3): 248–257.

Thiele, Jonathan E., Michael S. Pratte, and Jeffrey N. Rouder. 2011. On perfect working-memory performance with large numbers of items. *Psychonomic Bulletin & Review* 18 (5): 958–963.

Thomas, Margaret H., and Alvin Y. Wang. 1996. Learning by the keyword mnemonic: Looking for long-term benefits. *Journal of Experimental Psychology. Applied* 2 (4): 330–342.

Tucker, G. Richard. 1999. A global perspective on bilingualism and bilingual education. Center for Applied Linguistics. http://www.cal.org/resource-center/briefs-digests/digests.

Tulving, Endel, and Donald M. Thomson. 1973. Encoding specificity and retrieval processes in episodic memory. *Psychological Review* 80 (5): 352–373.

Tversky, Amos, and Daniel Kahneman. 1973. Availability: A heuristic for judging frequency and probability. *Cognitive Psychology* 5 (2): 207–232.

Twain, Mark. (1880)2010. *The Awful German Language*. http://kanalisation.ernstchan.com/b/src/1400909306066.pdf/Mark%20Twain%20Awful%20Broschuere.pdf.

Verhaeghen, Paul. 2011. Aging and executive control: Reports of a demise greatly exaggerated. *Current Directions in Psychological Science* 20 (3): 174–180.

Vygotsky, Lev S. 1980. *Mind in Society: The Development of Higher Psychological Processes*. Cambridge, MA: Harvard University Press.

Walker, W. Richard, John J. Skowronski, and Charles P. Thompson. 2003. Life is pleasant—and memory helps to keep it that way! *Review of General Psychology* 7 (2): 203–210.

Wang, Hui-Xin, Anita Karp, Bengt Winblad, and Laura Fratiglioni. 2002. Late-life engagement in social and leisure activities is associated with a decreased risk of dementia: A longitudinal study from the Kungsholmen project. *American Journal of Epidemiology* 155 (12): 1081–1087.

Weingartner, Herbert, Wolansa Adefris, James E. Eich, and Dennis L. Murphy. 1976. Encoding-imagery specificity in alcohol state-dependent learning. *Journal of Experimental Psychology: Human Learning and Memory* 2 (1): 83–87.

Weiss, Michael W., Sandra E. Trehub, and E. Glenn Schellenberg. 2012. Something in the way she sings: Enhanced memory for vocal melodies. *Psychological Science* 23 (10): 1074–1078.

Whorf, Benjamin Lee, and Stuart Chase. 1956. *Language, Thought, and Reality: Selected Writings of Benjamin Lee Whorf*. Ed. John B. Carroll. Cambridge, MA: MIT Press.

Wood, Benjamin. 2011. The Iron Lady: Meryl Streep says accents are the easiest thing she does. *Entertainment Weekly*, December 7. http://insidemovies.ew.com/2011/12/07/meryl-streep-iron-lady-panel/.

Würtz, Elizabeth. 2006. Intercultural communication on websites: A cross-cultural analysis of websites from high-context cultures and low-context cultures. *Journal of Computer-Mediated Communication* 11 (1): 274–299.

Yerkes, Robert M., and John D. Dodson. 1908. The relation of strength of stimulus to rapidity of habit-formation. *Journal of Comparative Neurology and Psychology* 18:459–482.

Zechmeister, Eugene B., Andrea M. Chronis, William L. Cull, Catherine A. D'Anna, and Noreen A. Healy. 1995. Growth of a functionally important lexicon. *Journal of Literacy Research* 27 (2): 201–212.

Zell, Ethan, and Zlatan Krizan. 2014. Do people have insight into their abilities? A metasynthesis. *Perspectives on Psychological Science* 9 (2): 111–125.

Zimmer, Ben. 2010. GHOTI. *New York Times Magazine*, June 25. http://www.nytimes.com/2010/06/27/magazine/27FOB-onlanguage-t.html?_r=0.

# Index